How to Like Paul Again

"This small book is the best thing I have ever read on Paul written for a non-academic audience. In a winsome vernacular voice, Gempf introduces us to a Paul we can approach and admire, if not hug. The book's only shortcoming – it ended too soon. How rare to find a book short enough to be read in an evening, profound enough to be savored for a lifetime."

Leonard Sweet, best-selling author, professor (Drew University, George Fox University), and chief contributor to sermons.com

"Conrad Gempf has the gift of taking complex tasks and making them seem simple, enjoyable and relevant; he has done it again with this little book. Illustrating his method with Galatians, 1 Corinthians and Philemon, Gempf shows how to interpret individual statements in Paul's letters in light of their whole contexts. Paul's true passions, priorities and tact clearly emerge in ways that may surprise even long-time Bible readers. Novice interpreters can scarcely dare ignore this gem of a guide."

Craig L Blomberg, Distinguished Professor of New Testament, Denver Seminary

"In this vital, edgy, intensely readable book, Conrad writes as a scholar with a winsome smile and a generous heart. The warmth of the book thaws the awkward frostiness that currently exists around Paul, and we're invited again to discover what true passion and radical commitment really looks like. I like Paul more now. And I like this book a lot."

Jeff Lucas, author, speaker, broadcaster

"Conrad extends an invitation for us to see past our judgements and confusion and access something of who Paul really was. Accept that invitation and you'll find fascinating insights which may change not only your attitude to Paul, but the way you read the whole Bible. This is a gem of a book for individual or group study; I highly recommend it."

Mike Pilavachi, Soul Survivor

"Gempf is a genius at opening God's word, and raising our level of understanding, so that the Bible speaks directly to our contemporary context. This book helped me not only to like Paul more, but want to be more like him."

Anna Robbins, Associate Professor of Theology, Academic Dean, Director of Doctoral Studies, Acadia Divinity College, Nova Scotia, Canada

"Conrad Gempf is an exceptional communicator and a sideways thinker. He's also effortlessly cool. Thousands of people have bene-fited from his insights, his occasionally quirky way of seeing things, and his grasp of Scripture. In this new book – which is unafraid to tackle one of the biggest elephants in the crypt – Conrad demon-strates that he shares a gift with greats like Malcolm Gladwell: he can make the complex, comprehensible – and what's more, enjoyable. Conrad sees Paul as one of the great misunderstood men of history, and sets about re-examining and reinterpreting him for the modern church. What he uncovers will surprise, entertain and challenge you. By the end of it, you'll have learned to like Paul again. You might even want to be a little more like Paul."

Martin Saunders, Editor of Youthwork *magazine*

"For some folk, there is an appalling amount of Paul in the NT. Paul, they think, is at turns inflammatory, infuriating, incomprehensible, and insensitive. If you are one of those people, then Conrad Gempf's new reader-friendly guide on how to learn to like Paul again (or for the first time) is just the book for you. As Gempf ably shows, Paul may be politically incorrect, but anti-Jewish, anti-women, anti-love, or antinomian he is not. It's time to put away the banner that reads 'Back to Jesus . . . and Away with Paul'."

Ben Witherington, III, Amos Professor for Doctoral Studies,
Asbury Theological Seminary;
Doctoral Faculty St. Andrews University, Scotland

How to Like Paul Again

The Apostle You Never Knew

Conrad Gempf

Authentic

22 21 20 19 18 17 16 15 14 13   11 10 9 8 7 6 5 4 3 2
Reprinted 2013
First published 2013 by Authentic Media Limited
52 Presley Way, Crownhill, Milton Keynes, MK8 0ES.
www.authenticmedia.co.uk

British Library Cataloguing in Publication Data
A catalogue record for this book is available from the British Library
ISBN 978-1-78078-061-0
978-1-78078- 092-4 (e-book)

Cover Design by Brett Jordan (www.x1.ltd.uk)
Printed and bound by CPI Group (UK) Ltd., Croydon, CR0 4YY

Contents

This is for you teachers,
especially if you're one who, like Paul,
teaches to the heart first of all.

Foreword

Sometimes people just decide not to like something or someone; these used to be known as people "up the Miff Tree." Although other antique metaphors like "up a creek without a paddle" are still with us, "up the Miff Tree" is no longer in circulation, even though in its time it inspired many poems, songs, and even whole books.

Pastors used to pass on this old metaphor furtively from one to another. Whether they recognize the metaphor or not, every pastor knows the Miff Tree. This skeletal, leafless tree has perched in it some gruesome birds whose feet have been trampled on, whose feelings have been hurt, whose feathers have been ruffled. These are people who once "served" the church until they flew up into the Miff Tree. Now they sit and stew, miffed and huffy, waiting like vultures for the first sign of weakness and blood. Pastors learned to treat people "up the Miff Tree" with long arms and kid gloves.

The Miff Tree

(Anonymous)

Who has not heard of the Miff Tree?
The most common thing under the sun.
It grows without soil, like an air plant;
And nearly everybody has one.
It is easy to raise, it is started

From a little slip of the tongue;
And almost before you know it,
To giant proportions has grown.

It is handy to climb up into,
When your feelings suffer a bump;
When the stock of your patience
Meets with a sudden slump.

Its odor is not very inviting;
But for that nobody cares.
For when you climb up in a Miff Tree,
You always put on airs.

Sometimes a great, thrifty Miff Tree,
Will grow right in the church;
And though it looks rather peculiar,
There's many a one on its perch.

If you would destroy a Miff Tree,
Keep humility growing close by:
It drives all poison out of the air;
And the tree will wither and die.

Or if you would live in a place,
Where the Miff Tree never does grow;
Just move into the Lord's dovecote,
Where his saints consort here below.

No one has a bigger Miff Tree than the Apostle Paul. Up the tree are dignitaries like Thomas Jefferson, who called Paul "the first corrupter of the doctrines of Jesus," and luminaries like George Bernard Shaw, who denounced Paul for turning Christianity into "Crosstianity." Both conservatives and liberals jostle each other for space on the branches of the Miff Tree. Conservatives don't trust Paul because he seems more responsible for shaping Christianity than Jesus – not to mention that Paul was never trained by the disciples, the men who walked, talked, and broke bread with our Savior, but who received his knowledge from "revelations." And liberals don't like Paul, because of what he said about women and sex. They blame Paul, not Jesus, for bad treatment of Jewish people. Despite writing the most eloquent and romantic love letter in existence (the "greatest of all" love chapter of 1 Corinthians 13), Paul has proved to be not quite the charmer for women, who fill the tree with chatter and catcalls of patriarchy. Scholars resent the way Paul gets credit for things that aren't his. Paul's "letter to the Hebrews" presents some difficulties, for example: it's not a letter, it's not written to Hebrews, and it's not written by Paul.

Conrad Gempf makes it as easy as possible for all Paul's haters and hurters to climb down from the Miff Tree. Paul's genius with metaphor (for example, the church as the "body of Christ") established the profound grammar from which various traditions of the faith were conjugated, and even brought healing (see the fight over *filioque* ["and the Son"] and *azyma* [yeastless bread]). As Gempf shows in his compulsively readable prose, the stern, forbidding Paul is actually quite lovable and approachable. Paul even contends that the nature of ministry is to see that "love may abound more and more in real knowledge and all discernment" (Philippians 1:9), not how this is to be done. The technologies of truth, the apps of "abounding," the means of meaning, are various for Paul. But love is the bottom line.

If you start reading this book already up the Miff Tree with Paul, swallow hard and brace yourself. You're about ready to hit the ground. And when you do, you'll get up saying with Paul that in Christ "we live, and move, and exist" (Acts 17:28).

Leonard Sweet

Foreword

Leonard Sweet, E. Stanley Jones professor of evangelism, Drew University, distinguished visiting professor, George Fox University, president emeritus, United Theological Seminary, chief contributor to sermons.com, and best-selling author.

Acknowledgements

It has been my incredible good fortune to have been blessed with wonderful teachers through my life, especially, but not only, the encouraging Marlene Thomas and Harold O'Cleppo, the enlightening Lloyd Carr and Marvin Wilson, the inspiring Howard Kee and Paul Sampley, and the incomparable Howard Marshall. Pride of place in this volume surely must go to Paul Sampley who changed my view of Paul forever by showing me Philemon and graciously pulling his playful punches while we argued about 1 Corinthians for weeks. This book would not have been written without him.

I'm very grateful to people in publishing who've worked with me on the idea of the book and the book itself. Stan Gundry, Ian Matthews, Tony Collins, Claire Musters, and all the people who said Yes and No and Maybe along the way. Especially, though, I'm grateful to my editor Amy Boucher Pye who has a way of magically making you want to rewrite a section for the tenth time, trying to "make it sing."

A fantastic group of friends read various chapters and drafts and made wonderfully useful suggestions along the way. They include colleagues and family and students. Brett Jordan, who also designed the cover, and Antony Billington, whose heart is even bigger than his brain, read chapters as they were produced and were willing to tell me what they liked and didn't like, and that meant the world to me. And among those who read chapters or the whole manuscript and helped me re-think were: Anna Robbins, John Wilks, Graham McFarlane, Rick Riggall, Robin Sanderson, Kathryn Pole, Steve Creamer, and

Acknowledgements

Lucy Mills. Thank you, one and all. If you find something in this book that irritates you, chances are that one of these people tried their darndest to make me change it and I didn't. Write a note to them so they can tell me "Told you so!"

And, of course, special thanks to my family for their patience and encouragement.

Many groups have sat through taught presentations of this material and I've always grown as a result of their reactions and comments. If you attended one of the BA classes, evening classes, men's breakfasts, or dinner theatre presentations, thank you. A special thank you to Deeside Christian Fellowship near Aberdeen, where I first looked at these three epistles together.

For Group Study

Lots of people use books like mine as the basis for small group studies. In order to facilitate that, I've included a few questions at the end of each of the chapters. You will probably want to read more than one short chapter a week, so here are a few suggestions of reading schemes you might want to try.

If you have four weeks, try this:

1) 1 2 3
2) 4 5 6
3) 7 8 9 10 11
4) 12 13 14 15

If you have six weeks try this:

1) 1 2 3
2) 4 5 6
3) 7 8 9
4) 10 11
5) 12 13
6) 14 15

If you have five weeks, try this:

1) 1 2 3
2) 4 5 6
3) 7 8 9
4) 10 11
5) 12 13 14 15

If seven weeks, try this:

1) 1 2
2) 3 4
3) 5 6
4) 7 8 9
5) 10 11
6) 12 13
7) 14 15

If you have longer than seven weeks, think about adding your own Bible study of another short epistle after my book – Philippians or 1 Thessalonians might be good choices.

PART I:

Introduction

– 1 –

Not Mr. Nice Guy

Don't, Don't, Don't

Sam Jones (not his real name) plays drums – and, rarely, the accordion – in the worship band. "On fire for the Lord" could describe him. He's always talking to his friends about God, and he's very active in the youth group. During talks at conferences and sometimes even during sermons, he takes notes in a little book. He reads his Bible pretty regularly, especially the New Testament.

He loves the Lord. But he doesn't really like Paul.

"The epistles have some great passages, like about fruits of the Spirit, spiritual gifts and that; I believe that God did great things through Paul – but he's not a guy I think I'd get on with. He's just the kind of Christian that people object to – full of don't do this and don't do that; so into authority and stuff. Don't, don't, don't."

Sound familiar? For some years now, I've discovered that many of the students in my classes, and many of the people in groups to whom I speak, don't like Paul. It doesn't seem to matter whether they've read a lot of his letters. Often it's not a reasoned thing. They just don't like Paul.

Maybe you're one of those people. Maybe someone bought you this book because you don't like Paul anymore. Maybe you got this book because you don't like Paul but feel you should. Maybe you never liked Paul. Maybe you think he's okay, but want to appreciate him more. Well, if any of those things are true, this book is for you. Because here's the thing: I've grown to love Paul; in fact, I now think he's an absolute genius. But I'm also extremely glad that he isn't my boss. I have no doubt that he was one of the most difficult people to work with in the history of the world.

What Makes Paul So Difficult?

Ask people *why* they don't like Paul and a lot of times even those who answer honestly will answer wrongly. What I mean by that is that they will inadvertently answer the wrong question. You ask, "Why do you dislike Paul?", but many will answer as if the question was actually, "Where do you disagree with Paul?" These days perhaps the most commonly cited disagreements concern gender and sexuality. That's understandable. People can get into very heated discussions about Paul in relation to these things, while at the same time admitting that they don't fully understand what Paul was intending to teach. That also is understandable; after all, Paul was writing in an ancient language and in an era of social upheaval. He was himself a mixture of two backgrounds – Roman citizen and trained Pharisaic Jew. And those two backgrounds were nearly as strange to each other as both are strange to us.

But, hang on a second. Disagreeing about something isn't really a good reason for disliking someone, is it? Don't we all have friends who we love to bits even though they hold some opinion we know is just dumb, dumb, dumb? And, similarly, isn't it easy to think of people who agree with you on issues, but with whom you just don't click?

More than issues, we should steer by attitudes, motivations, values, and priorities when forming an opinion of a person. Those are the things that matter. But it's hard to figure out that stuff about someone without getting to know them.

There's a saying that you shouldn't criticize another person until you've walked a mile in their moccasins. In giving us epistles – letters – rather than a theological textbook, the Bible invites us to take that walk and see what Paul writes not as pronouncement but as reply.

Reply? Reply to what? Aren't you curious?

If you're really going to dislike Paul, don't dislike him for his views on particular issues. This is especially true if the issues are hotspots for you personally – not for him or the people whose questions he writes to answer.

If you're really going to dislike Paul, dislike him instead for his attitudes and values once you find out what they are. Too often, we assume we know what they are. For instance, the novelist and essayist Fay Weldon was once asked to write an introduction to 1 Corinthians. Naturally, she assumed that Paul was writing an essay or treatise rather than a letter, and she assumed that she could deduce from that one letter Paul's overall attitude and values. She found Paul arrogant and authoritative; she found a bully who treated his readers as if they were children. I think you'll see, even before you finish reading this book, not only that she was very wrong, but also why she made the mistake that she made. Here's a hint: she "knows" she doesn't like him . . . but she doesn't really know him.

Paul and His Colleagues

People today find it difficult to like Paul. I get that. But, you know, it isn't as if Paul got a place in the Bible because no one till you, Sam Jones (not his real name), and Fay Weldon realized he was annoying. Some of the people who knew him best had trouble with him as well. I'm not sure whether the author meant this or not, but Acts 9:30 and 31 always make me laugh: "They [the believers] took [Paul] down to Caesarea and sent him off to Tarsus. *Then* the church throughout Judea, Galilee and Samaria enjoyed a time of peace." [Emphasis mine] But there is evidence that is clearer.

Find Paul hard to understand sometimes? So did Peter and his friends.

Listen to Peter sympathizing with early Christians who tried to read Paul's letters: "Our Lord's patience means salvation, just as our dear brother Paul also wrote you with the wisdom that God gave him." (Should we read this "with that measure of wisdom God gave him" – as in "He's trying his best . . ."?) The text of 2 Peter continues: "He writes the same way in all his letters, speaking in them of these matters. His letters contain some things that are hard to understand" (2 Peter 3:15–16). And these were people who understood Greek.

Find Paul wordy and boring? So did his congregations.

One of Paul's closest allies was the person who wrote both the Gospel of Luke and the book of Acts. He found Paul such a great man that he spent more than half of his second volume chronicling Paul's travels and life's work. But he didn't neglect to show the "bad" side of Paul. He chose to include some stories that Paul himself must have cringed to have aired. One of the favorites has to be a memorable evening in Troas: "Paul spoke to the people and, because he intended to leave the next day, kept on talking until midnight. There were many lamps in the upstairs room where we were meeting. Seated in a window was a young man named Eutychus, who was sinking into a deep sleep as Paul talked on and on. When he was sound asleep, he fell to the ground from the third story" (Acts 20:7–9). This story has a happy ending, but not before we get the message that Paul had a lot to say – sometimes more than his hearers could cope with.

Find Paul aggravating or infuriating? So did his fellow workers.

Among the first Christians, you couldn't find a sweeter, more likeable guy than Joseph, also called Barnabas. In Acts 4:36–7 he sold his stuff to help out his fellow Christians. And we're not talking about giving up his vintage *Star Trek* DVDs or even his CD collection; he was selling off his front garden! Other Christian leaders got nicknames like "Rock" (Peter), "the Sons of Thunder" (James and John), or "Stumpy Fingers" (as the Church Fathers tell us the John Mark who wrote Mark's Gospel was called); Barnabas earned himself the nickname "the Son of Encouragement." Everybody liked Barnabas.

And he certainly appears to have fulfilled the role of encourager for Paul as well. The rabidly anti-Christian Saul had become a believer in chapter 9 of Acts, but many in the church were still suspicious of him. They thought Saul was trying to infiltrate in order to root out and arrest the ringleaders. Guess who took the risk and brought Saul into the fold? "[Saul] tried to join the disciples, but they were all afraid of him, not believing that he really was a disciple. But Barnabas took him and brought him to the apostles" (Acts 9:26–7). I love that phrase in the last sentence: "But Barnabas . . ." So it was the Son of Encouragement who gathered Paul under his wing and brought him into communion with the larger church.

Everybody likes Barnabas and Barnabas likes everybody. But look what happens with him and Paul. You'll find another "but Barnabas" moment a few chapters later. Remember "Stumpy Fingers" John Mark? In Acts 13:13, he bailed out of traveling with Barnabas and Paul. Paul was not pleased. In Acts 15:37, Barnabas tried to bring John Mark back to Paul as he'd done earlier, bringing Paul to the apostles. But this attempted rapprochement turned to disaster. We read in 15:38–40: ". . . They had such a sharp disagreement that they parted company. Barnabas took Mark . . . but Paul chose Silas and left." How prickly must Paul have been to get into a fight with The Son of Encouragement? – the person who'd helped *him* out not so very long ago?

But here's the strange thing; seriously, stop for a second and think about this: everybody likes Barnabas, right? So why is the New Testament chock full of letters by this prickly Paul and not by cuddly Barnabas? Wouldn't you rather read the encouragement of Barnabas?

It's no mistake. Paul is a genius, someone you'll be glad is on your side. *Like* is not too strong a word. I know you don't believe it yet. The thing is, you have to get to know him. And to do that, you have to know what he was like before he was a Christian. So next we'll look at this bright, up-and-coming winner of the Young Pharisee of the Decade Award and how his post-University bid for independence went totally (and ironically) wrong. So kick off your shoes and let's test-drive some moccasins.

Questions for Discussion or Reflection

1. Why might some people dislike Paul? Can reasons be sorted into good reasons and bad reasons?

2. Do you think we have different reasons for liking people who are public figures and for people we encounter personally?

3. Has it ever happened to you that someone you initially had a strong dislike for turned out to be a wonderful person after all? What triggered such a reversal of your opinion?

– 2 –

Kicking against the Goads
(Whatever That Means . . .)

I wonder if you remember much about the story of Paul's call or conversion on the road to Damascus. On the way there, he was knocked off his donkey and onto his . . . well, knocked off his donkey. There was a light so powerful that it blinded him for days. And there was a voice so powerful that it changed him forever.

Like James Earl Jones, a deep voice said "Saul, Saul, why do you persecute me? It is hard for you to kick against the goads" (Acts 26:14).

Okay, kick against the *what*?

Very soon I'll come back to that. First let me explain why the voice *didn't* call him by his name, Paul, and then what he was doing on that road. Because one way or another, he really shouldn't have been there.

Paul or Saul?

Essentially, the voice called him Saul because that was Paul's name. His other name.

Yes, well, *one* of his other names. As well as his Jewish name, chances are he would have had one of those triple-barreled Roman names, like Marcus Didius Falco. One of his would have been Paulus. We have no record of the other two.

Often one or two of the three names take priority. For example, most people only know two of Gaius Julius Caesar's names, and only one of Marcus Junius Brutus'. And the New Testament also uses two names for lots of other characters. Sometimes Peter is called by the Greco-Roman Petros or Peter and other times by the Semitic Cephas (remember this name as we'll come across it again later).

Unexpectedly, it isn't at his conversion that Paul changed his name, but rather he began using his Roman name later, when he took up the challenge of his calling: to be the apostle to the Gentiles. Look for yourself: the Damascus road thing happens in Acts 9, but he seems to have gone by the name Saul until partway into the first missionary journey, Acts 13.

Incidentally, Saul/Paul wasn't born in Jerusalem. He hailed from a place called Tarsus, which was a well-known university town in the first century. He was born Jewish, of course, but in the Gentile world. In fact, according to Acts, he was born a Roman citizen. This gave him a trump card in the Empire, which he occasionally played (see Acts 22:25–9).

Our Saul was no secularized, nominal Jew, though. It was for the sake of his religious education that he was sent to Jerusalem as a young man. He apparently had relatives in the holy city (see Acts 23:16); perhaps he went to live with them. And in Jerusalem, as we shall see shortly, he not only succeeded but excelled at the feet of a very important and impressive Pharisee teacher.

Not having been born in Jerusalem would have been a disadvantage, but perhaps not as much as you'd think. There were Jews settled all over the Roman Empire, with cities like Alexandria in North Africa being important centers of Jewish culture and thought. The great Jewish philosophical writer Philo hailed from Alexandria rather than Jerusalem, for instance.

Evidence in Paul's own letters, as well as the book of Acts, points to his deep involvement in Pharisaic Judaism. In Galatians 1:14 he writes: "I was advancing in Judaism beyond many of my own age . . . and was extremely zealous for the traditions of my fathers." Paul the

Christian *still* thought of himself as a Pharisee (as did other Christians in Acts 15:5). In Philippians 3:4–5 he says: "If someone else thinks they have reasons to put confidence in the flesh, I have more: circumcised on the eighth day, of the people of Israel, of the tribe of Benjamin, a Hebrew of Hebrews; in regard to the law, a Pharisee." He didn't leave behind his old name for a new one; he didn't cast off his Jewishness for a new religion. Even in the midst of his ministry, he did not write of his Judaism as something he'd left behind – Christianity did not replace Judaism.

So what does he mean when, later in the Philippians passage, 3:7–8, he takes an emphatically negative view of his accomplishments? "Whatever were gains to me I now consider loss," "I consider everything a loss," and "I consider [these things] garbage."

Some passages in a speech in Acts give us the clues: "I am a Jew." Paul says in the present tense in Acts 22:3. But then he continues with a *past* tense "Under Gamaliel [I] was thoroughly trained . . . [and] was just as zealous for God as any of you."

In the Philippians passage, again, Paul regards himself as a Jew. It is his accomplishments in Judaism he regards as rubbish now, not Judaism itself. He regards his achievements as rubbish *in comparison* to Christ. That last bit is important. He isn't saying, "Now that I know the truth, I'm able to see my great accomplishments were actually rubbish," but rather "Compared to the truth I now know, the greatest accomplishments of the old paradigm seem like rubbish."

It's a paradigm shift, but it's not a simple replacement. To draw analogies from the world of science, it's not that he was highly trained in astrology and now sees that all his accomplishments were internally flawed and objectively worthless; rather it is as if he was highly trained in classical Newtonian physics and suddenly discovered (or been discovered by) quantum physics. The shift opens up a totally new understanding of the universe in a way that only makes the old invalid if the old claims to be all there is.

It was Paul's accomplishments that he counted as rubbish. What he gave up to become what we would call "a Christian" was not his Judaism but his career. He let go a promising, high-flying career. And he did so just at the moment when he was about to pull off the career move of his life – a political maneuver that would redefine him in the mold of a Jewish leader of great renown, as we'll see in the next section.

What's He Doing on the Road?

Why was Paul there? This seems a simple question to answer: because he was on his way to persecute Christians. But hang on. Why should *he* be doing that? Was he some member of the Temple guard? Some Pharisee Fixer? *Who* was he?

In this section, I'm speculating somewhat. I think this reconstruction of Saul's career makes a lot of sense, but not all scholars would agree with it. See what you think . . .

The big clue is that when Paul talks about those days, he slips into a way of talking about himself that only a young man, like a student or recent graduate, would use: "I was advancing in Judaism beyond many of *my own age*" he wrote (Galatians 1:14, emphasis mine). In a speech in the book of Acts, Paul defines his pre-Christian days by talking about where he studied and with whom (Acts 22:3). We are also told that the Saul who was present at the persecution of Stephen was a *young* man (Acts 7:58).

He was an advanced student and his mentor was Gamaliel, a rabbi so famous that he is still revered today. The Jewish Mishnah, written centuries later, says, "Since Rabban Gamaliel the Elder died there has been no more reverence for the law, and purity and abstinence died out at the same time" (m. Sotah 9.15). Saul's mentor was the most famous rabbi of his generation and Saul was his up-and-coming protégé.

This was still forty years before Rome would sack Jerusalem and destroy the Temple. There was peace with Rome, albeit an uneasy one. But Saul, remember, was not only a highly trained and promising Pharisaic rabbi, but also a Roman citizen. What might have happened if such a rising star had succeeded his mentor and taken a place at the ruling council, the Sanhedrin?

When we meet Saul in Acts, he *is* young, as we saw. He hasn't quite got enough credentials of his own. When he wants to go to Damascus to persecute Christians, he knows that his own authority is insufficient. But this is the mark of his position: he needs letters of recommendation, it is true, but he is well enough connected and thought of that he is able to get them (Acts 9:1–2; cf. 22:5).

What I'm driving at is this: Saul was a young man with a future. The outlook must have seemed not only secure but positively brimming with potential. It wasn't as if he came from obscurity. He did not join the Christians in order to become a large fish in a small pond. He was headed to become a very large fish in a very large pond. The teachings and reputation of Gamaliel stretch into the twenty-first century. The words of Saul of Tarsus could have been similarly immortalized; if he had been left to himself, orthodox Jews today might be speaking about Saul of Tarsus with the same respect as they speak of Gamaliel the Wise or Johanan ben Zakkai or Honi the Circle Drawer. (Or maybe slightly more respect than Honi the Circle Drawer, actually.)

One problem though: when your mentor stands as tall in the spotlight as Gamaliel does, how do you get yourself out from under his shadow? When the time comes and you're done with your studies, you need to make a name for yourself. In our day, you'd have to publish some major work of your own, perhaps disagreeing with your teacher. Or in a different field, pull off some daring acquisition/merger that was unforeseen by your former mentors.

This, I think, is the explanation for why Saul of Tarsus was on that road persecuting. The book of Acts tells us that Gamaliel himself took a very laid-back position on what Jews should do to stop the Christians. In Acts 5, his attitude is shown to be that if it were from God no one could stop it, but if, as he thought was the case, it wasn't from God, it would fizzle out like all the other mistaken movements and messiahs. No persecution, no fuss, no stress: just let them alone.

That was the pronouncement of Gamaliel in chapter 5. But it is clear that at least by the time of chapter 7, this was no longer the view of the Sanhedrin – their anger and impatience boiled over into murder with the stoning of Stephen. And so it was, I think, that the young and ambitious star pupil of Gamaliel saw a way to differentiate himself from his teacher and make a name for himself in a way that would earn the gratitude of the current leadership: he would take charge of handling the Christian heresy. He would show his difference from his master by a move that would make him immensely popular with everyone else. Brilliant.

At the stoning of Stephen, Acts portrays Saul in a minor role – a young man, holding the coats of the Sanhedrin members taking full part in the execution. But look: by the beginning of chapter 8, it is he who is breathing murderous threats. Then in the ninth chapter he will lead this expedition to Damascus, but, as I said, he has insufficient authority to just do so – he needs to obtain a reference letter from someone established. And here's another interesting thing: he's well connected enough that he is able to accomplish this. His recommendation comes not from his mentor or his own party, but from the leader of the rival party, the Sadducees – from the High Priest himself. Saul of Tarsus is rising up, in the transition stage between promising grad student and accomplished leader in his own right.

Now I am not suggesting that his opposition to Christianity was merely a cynical opportunistic stance. Belief that there is only one god is not unusual today but it certainly was then, and Jewish self-identity centered on the one-ness and uniqueness of God. What Christians believed about Jesus and the way that they worshiped him, from the earliest days, would have filled a zealous Jew with the outrage and anger one feels not about an opponent but about a traitor. Saul would have hated Christianity. But he rose up from a minor role to a major one, and at a time that served his career well.

At least, it *would* have served his career well if it hadn't been for an irritating intervention.

About That Goad

And so it was that a young Pharisee, whose master advocated taking no action, was initiating a major offensive, armed with letters of recommendation from the leading Sadducee on a mission to mop up a small group of heretics and return triumphant to a relieved and unified Jerusalem leadership. But before he could arrive there – while he was still on the road – he was intercepted. A bright light knocked him over and that voice came, calling his name and talking about goads.

A goad, in those days, was a stout, sharpened stick. You would use it to herd livestock. Animals like cows have such thick hides that you can't get their attention by tapping them on the shoulder. Even giving them a sharp slap won't be noticed. To get such an animal to notice you and the directions you're giving it, you have to deliver a blow that would injure a human being. A sharp stick dug into their backside might feel to them like a finger prodding our backs – enough to be noticed. And, repeated, enough of an irritation to force compliance. That's a goad.

This is what the voice from heaven was saying. "Who are you, sir?" asked Saul from the ground. "I am Jesus, whom you are persecuting," came the reply. Jesus was an irritant to Paul, and here he is learning what kind of irritant. It is not a parasite but a goad. Jesus is God's irritant. And this thick-skinned Pharisee trying to kickstart his career needed to learn that his future lay not in kicking against the irritant but in going along with it, where *it* wants him to go.

Saul never became the leading Jewish teacher of his day, as he might well have hoped to do. He never became President of the Sanhedrin as his master Gamaliel was said to have been. He didn't gain a comfortable apartment in the Temple quarters in Jerusalem, as his mentor may have had. He gave all that up. Think of that – leaving the firm, leaving the whole field, when your prospects for promotion are great. Instead he became a prisoner, spending many years in chains.

Neither did he ever become any sort of official leader of the Christian church. In Acts, both Peter and James are portrayed as the leaders, the authoritative voices. This may be hard for us to see. When we look back at that era, Paul seems to us like the most influential and prestigious of the bunch. You don't have to read far in Acts or in his letters before you are confronted with clear evidence that this wasn't so in his day. It wasn't his experience even in the local churches he founded, much less across the larger church.

By becoming a Christian apostle, Paul was *surrendering* position, and status, and authority, not gaining it. And, as a Pharisee steeped in traditions, the Christian Paul was relaxing his views on regulations and authority, not becoming more authoritative.

This helps me like him, but I don't expect it to have much effect on you yet. Seeing where he has come from and the choices he's made will help you understand what he's writing and why.

If Paul was a newspaper columnist or an essay writer, it would perhaps be the most important thing. But Paul wrote epistles. And that fact gives us other clues that are even more important in understanding his writings – that might be the key to liking him more. And that's what we'll look at next.

Questions for Discussion or Reflection

1. Paul was trained in Jerusalem to the highest level in Judaism. Peter was brought up in a village in Galilee, known by fellow Jews as "Galilee of the Gentiles." Why in the world did God make Paul the apostle to the Gentiles and Peter the apostle to the Jews?

2. Paul was an outspoken persecutor of the church at a time when it was dangerous to be a Christian. How hard it must have been for the Christians to trust him when he claimed to share their faith. Try to think of what situations today would be like that; can we even imagine such a thing in our safe, Western culture?

3. Have you known other Christians who have given up lucrative or high-status positions because of their faith? Spend a little time praying for them.

Reading Epistles as Letters

Flat Reading

Once upon a time, I used the Bible in a very flat way. If you'd asked me what my favorite book of the Bible was, I might not have been able to tell you. I wouldn't have really understood the question. I might have answered "the New Testament" or John 3 or Romans 10 – 14. I didn't understand that the Bible was made up of dozens of distinct books. I saw the Bible only as a single thing and written by a single author, God. And I thought it was written for me.

Now, in a way, I still believe this: the Bible is divinely inspired by God and of benefit for everyone, including me. The key error I made was thinking it was *only* that. People used to – only partially joking – refer to it as the User's Manual for Creation. And some of us went further. I saw it as the Troubleshooting Appendix of the User's Manual.

So, while I may not have had a favorite book of the Bible, I did have a favorite section of my Bible. It was in the back, after the book of Revelation. My King James version had a few pages called "What to Read When." I loved it. It listed modern-life situations and matched them with bits of Bible to read. There was a psalm for "When celebrating a birth"; a bit of Paul to read "When a loved one dies"; something else for "When you lose your job"; another passage for "When facing difficulties"; and something else to read "When disappointed in love." It was great. It helped me bypass all the irrelevant bits of God's word and get straight to the passage written for the situation I saw myself in. After a while, of course, my Bible, all by itself, naturally fell open to the well-used passage for "disappointed in love," but I still treasured the idea of "What to Read When."

It was a "flat" view of Scripture. And it was a selfish one. It was all and only about me; what's in it for me? If the Bible is anything like a relationship between God and me, then the relationship that I had was all about "using him."

But we would never do this with another human being, would we? If someone started telling you a story about something amazing that happened to them, would you say, "Yes, yes, yes . . . there was a horrible situation and people were in trouble, but can you just cut to the part of the story that's about me?"

Yet that's how many people who claim to love God treat the stories in the Bible. "Cut to the part that's about me." We call it relevance, but in fact what that means is: me me me; "Don't tell me about you, tell me about me." This is a bit of a hobbyhorse of mine. Let me rant about it a little bit more, by telling you a story.

Once upon a time, in a little town in Scotland, there lived a young man named Angus who was gifted in precisely those areas of math and business studies that qualified him as a financial genius. One day, he decided to travel to London to make his fortune.

Before he left he reassured his dear old mother: "Fear not, mother," he said, like the good fictional character he was, "When I return in twelve months I will have made my fortune and I will choose my bride." The problem was that there were two women Angus might marry, Fiona and Heather, and both certainly seemed smitten with him.

But off he went to London, minded to write to them both every week and choose between them when he returned.

Now at first, no one was certain how young Angus would get on. But any anxiety was misplaced, for he soon found a job near the center of the stock market business, and was quickly making a reputation for himself.

True to his plan, on Mondays he wrote to Fiona and on Wednesdays to Heather. And both women awaited and tore open their letters with great anticipation.

But there was a difference between them.

Fiona tore open the letter and read through every line, immersing herself in the details of Angus's life, trying to imagine what he must be feeling. For she truly loved the man, longed to be with him, and loved his letters for the token of contact that they were.

Heather, too, treasured the letters and pored over their contents, but with rather a different attitude. She too combed through each paragraph, but she did so sifting his words for clues about the markets. His moods and chance comments translated, for her, directly into mouse clicks as she instructed her PC to buy or sell or hold tight on the basis of her "insider information." And she gleaned enough to make a tidy sum.

Which woman do you think Angus should marry, especially if he thinks he's marrying for love?

If, like Heather, the only thing I care about is myself – relevance – then my reading of the Bible will be very flat.

But there is a way of taking the Bible personally without reading it selfishly. If you're like Fiona, when you talk with someone you love, you don't sort through what they say, listening to what is relevant and ignoring whatever is not. Because here is the key: *relevance* is not an unchangeable thing; relevance is not the ruler-standard against which everything is measured. Instead, *love* is the unchangeable thing. Allow love to determine what is relevant and what is not. Thus whatever the person you love is interested in *becomes* relevant to you. You want to know more and understand better.

Being interested in the other is the first step in getting past flat hearing and flat reading.

Three-Dimensional Reading

The alternative to "flat" is three-dimensional. Visually, our knowledge of the world comes from a two-dimensional image of it on our retinas. From this flat pattern of light, somehow, our minds are able to construct a 3D model of what we're seeing. If you've studied art, or the way that the brain processes vision, you will know that we use a variety of clues to help us perceive some things as popping forward and others as looming behind. Visual-perception clues are good analogies for how we can develop three-dimensional reading of texts like Paul's letters.

One of the most basic clues is simple perspective: we use things that overlap to help us determine what is background. Once you have a good sense of the background, it becomes easier to perceive other things as happening in front of it. This is no less true when reading Paul's letters. When we become aware of the situation behind the letters, we more easily see what it was that Paul himself was doing and saying.

Another very important clue is binocularity. We have two eyes in slightly different locations and these enable us to see things from two slightly different perspectives at the same time. You've done this experiment before, no doubt: hold a finger up in front of your face and look at it with first one eye open then the other. See how the object changes its location against the background? Move it further away from you and try again. Our brains automatically decode this difference, called *parallax*, into a sense of what is near and what is far. And, if the degree of parallax is changing, our brain knows whether something is moving toward or away from us. This type of clue is so important that when our eyes are tricked with special glasses we wind up ducking spears flung at us from cinema screens.

Similarly, we come to learn a lot about a biblical text when we learn to look at it from different stances. In its simplest form, you can see this from the way that I tended to only ask, "What can I learn about *my life* from this text?" That's a great question to ask of the text of the Bible. However, paradoxically, I find I learn even more about the answer to that question by also asking *other* questions, such as, "If I were one of the Galatians, what was I supposed to learn from the text?" Not because that's a better question – it isn't – but because it's a different question – because two eyes are better than one: binocularity.

A third clue, less important but still subtly useful, is texture. We can see the texture of things that are close to us in greater detail than that of things that are far away. How I've learned to incorporate what I call the "texture" of Scripture is harder to explain in the abstract. But it has to do with *how* the letters are written. For instance, when you sort the post, you know to read a letter differently when it's got a little window in the envelope with the address visible in there than when the envelope is handwritten and addressed to you. Even if the *content* of the address is exactly the same, the way that the content is presented gives you a message all its own, apart from content. As we look at the letters, I'll show you traces of these sorts of clues as well.

Other People's Mail . . . Not Lectures but Letters

So one day, Charlie Brown and Linus are walking home from church together. They're both wearing skinny ties like kids used to have to wear to church in the 1950s, even in comic strips. And Linus is pretty upset. His Sunday school teacher has started teaching his class about Paul's epistles. In the punch-line panel, there is a sort of resigned exasperation: "All these years . . . I've been reading someone else's mail!"

That's what they are. They're letters. And many of them were not originally written for everyone, but for the specific people they were addressed to. Isn't that strange?

If there was no New Testament, and God commissioned you or me to write one, there's no way that we would have chosen *this*. First you get four different versions of the same biography (Why? Why not assign one official biographer and ensure that he or she gets the story right?), then a book about his followers, other people's mail . . . and, as if that weren't enough, *then* the book of Revelation. Yikes.

You or I would have written a more systematic book: an encyclopedia or a wiki or a User's Manual with a Troubleshooting FAQ section. Why isn't it like that?

Maybe we get something added to the content by having it in the form – or with the texture – of other people's mail. If you believe that God is behind the writing of the Bible, the implication is that the inclusion of epistles is deliberate. It seems to me then, that that fact is part of God's communication, not incidental to it. We need to take the content seriously, but we also need to take them seriously *as letters*.

Several good things happen when you take this point to heart. First, the letters become more interesting to read. But second, and perhaps more importantly, you begin to hear an intonation – almost between the lines. You begin to sense the writers, the readers, and their ideas within the lines that are there.

Our perception of the meaning of language changes depending on the situation. Let me give you an example. Suppose you heard me say that my name was spelled, "G E M M M M P F." You'd think it a strange name and wonder what went wrong with the cover of this book. But suppose instead, you saw that I was on the telephone and took notice of the times I paused or shook my head: "G E M . . . M . . . M! . . . . . M! . . . PF." Can you hear how different that is? Something remarkable happens when you realize that that content is part of a conversation: First, you interpret the content differently and, second, you begin to sense what the other side of the conversation is like (in this case, the hearer is misunderstanding the letter M).

Here's How a Letter Reads

In fact, you can often tell a lot about the larger conversation by reading one side of it. I have some wonderful examples of this that I am forbidden from showing you, due to legal reasons of high finance, intellectual-property rights, California lawyers, and multinational corporations. So I've made one up that's typical of reply letters:

The Regency-General Hotel
Philadelphia
Ms. Olivia Crimler
Booking Manager

Ms. Christina Flynn
560 Oak Road,
Moor Park, New Jersey

Dear Ms. Flynn,

Thank you for considering The Regency-General Hotel. We are glad that you consider us "the venue of choice" for conducting your business negotiations. We take great pride in the atmosphere of relaxed elegance to which you refer.

I am pleased that you had the foresight to warn us about your unusual meetings. I'm afraid, however, that we cannot make exceptions to our basic dress code of casual formal for the meetings you have in mind. Dressing in costume would be disruptive to our other guests no matter where you sat in the public dining area.

Booking one of our private suites, however, would allow you to confine your appearance as George the Giant Frog to that private area. If this is something you are willing to consider, we would be glad to discuss the arrangements at your convenience.

All of us at The Regency-General Hotel wish you the best on all your business ventures and look forward to serving you in the future.

Sincerely,
Olivia Crimler

Often what makes responses to prank letters laugh-out-loud funny is imagining the situation into which the author puts his victims: the constraints of their jobs mean that they have to write a polite reply to even the most inane request because the letter writer might be serious and is a potential customer.

When you read this short letter, part of what makes you smile is that you learn about a lot more than the content of the letter. This effect is not unique to prank letter replies. There is so much you know now that you don't even know you know it. Obviously, you would learn from this letter, if this were real, that there is a Regency-General Hotel in Philadelphia. You would also learn that it is a formal place with an unwritten but enforced dress code. These things are stated in the letter. But you also learn things that aren't in the letter itself: does Ms. Flynn know Ms. Crimler? Having read the letter, you now know something about their previous relationship. Namely that it started with a letter from Ms. Flynn.

But not only do you know that there *was* a previous letter, if you think for a minute, you'll realize that you also know pretty much what must have been *in* that letter from Ms. Flynn. Sometimes, from a well-written reply, you can reconstruct the original down to the correct number of paragraphs, each dealing with the right subjects. In fact, in a letter like this, it's even possible that you have a better idea of what Ms. Flynn's letter was *really* about than Ms. Crimler did.

But even wilder, the knowledge that you glean is not only about the past, but also about the future. You also have some idea of what would happen if they met. You know about their personalities. And here's what I love the best . . . suppose I was able to include photographs of Chris Flynn and Olivia Crimler on the next page of this book. Do you have any doubt now that you would be able to tell me which picture was which – just from their body language and clothing, even if Ms. Flynn wasn't wearing her "George the Giant Frog" costume (which you probably realize she does not actually own anyway)? In some real but intangible way, you have come to *know* both of them.

All this because you read the letter *as a letter*. If your approach to reading this letter was the same as your usual approach to reading the Bible, you'd be in a very different position.

"Today's reading is from the first Epistle of Crimler, chapter 2, verse 12: 'we would be glad to discuss the arrangements at your convenience.' Here endeth the epistle reading."

Read it that way and it's flat advice. Nobody's drawn in to what's going on. Nobody laughs. Read it as a letter and vistas open up in many directions. And so do understanding and smiles.

Now *this* is what I want to teach you to do with Paul's letters. Wouldn't *that* be great? To read each letter *as* a letter and find that you know Paul – and the Galatians – better? If you are ever going to like Paul better than you do now, I think the change will come through getting to know him by reading his letters in this kind of light. Read on.

Questions for Discussion or Reflection

1. Did you start, as I did, with a very flat view of Scripture? Can you remember any time when an overly simplistic reading of a verse out of context led you astray?

2. Can it be that the Christian Scriptures are only for people with enough brainpower to think their way into the backgrounds and contexts of the letters? How might God expect people without high intelligence, or illiterate people, to relate to him through Scripture? How do children relate to God through the Bible? How do you resolve the tension between our need to be like little children (Matthew 18:5) and the biblical injunctions to be more mature in understanding (1 Corinthians 14:20; cf. 1 Corinthians 3:1–2)?

3. Why in the world would God give us a Bible made up of other people's mail?

PART II:

Chill Out – Galatians

– 4 –

"Those People" Hijack Galatia

When we read a book called *The Lion, the Witch, and the Wardrobe*, we rather expect to find out about a lion, a witch, and a wardrobe. So why is it that we almost never read Paul's letter to the Galatians looking to find out more about Paul and the Galatians? What was it about their lives together that got the letter to the Galatians into the New Testament?

The plotline behind Galatians is fairly simple once you realize it's a triangle. As well as Paul, who wrote the letter, and the community of Galatian (non-Jewish) Christians who received the letter, there is also a group of other (Jewish Christian) teachers who come to Galatia from elsewhere. Paul refers to them as "those people." So the Galatians started out on Paul's side, and then the other teachers came along after he was gone. Their teaching disagreed with Paul's and they started convincing the Galatians that their way was right and Paul's was wrong. Paul wrote this letter to the Galatians in reply. Simple. And simple to find out about, if you know where to look.

When you read this letter as a genuine letter – something written by someone to someone else – you'll find clues about the relationship between Paul and the Galatians scattered all through it. You just have to let yourself be interested in that and not blip over those parts.

How did Paul meet the Galatians? The clues are here: "It was because of an illness that I first preached the gospel to you, and even though my illness was a trial to you . . . you welcomed me as if I were an angel of God" (Galatians 4:13–14).

Here it is – laid out for us in a nutshell. Paul made a stop, perhaps even a detour, in Galatia, because he was ill. He found the people there welcoming, they comforted him in his illness, and he shared the gospel with them.

Those People

After Paul left, other teachers visited the impressionable Galatians, and the Galatians welcomed *them* as well. But the new teachers didn't agree with Paul. So the passage continues: "Have I now become your enemy . . . ? Those people are zealous to win you over, but for no good. What they want is to alienate you from us, so that you may have zeal for them" (Galatians 4:16–17).

This is no dispassionate timeline of events. Can't you sense it from these words? – Paul's raking over the past *because* he's upset and angry. "Those People."

Now, if this was any other book – if you were reading to understand the story rather than to find clues about how to apply it to your life – you'd be trying to discover what the other teachers were teaching that made Paul so angry and what it was about them that could drive a wedge between Paul and the community he founded. Well, remember the telephone conversation where I spelled my name? Remember the repetition and frustration in my voice as I repeated the letter M? That signals to you where it was that the person on the other end was stuck. Well . . . think of Paul as being on the telephone as you read these verses from Galatians: "Evidently some people are throwing you into confusion and are trying to pervert the gospel of Christ. But even if we or an angel from heaven should preach a gospel other than the one we preached to you, let them be under God's curse!" (Galatians 1:7–8).

There's an unmistakable "telephone tone" in his voice: "I don't care *who* these people think they are, even if they're angels from heaven."

These people have some claim to authority. Are they claiming angelic authority? Probably not, because of the repetition that comes just a few sentences later. Paul provides clues about what authority these people claimed: "The gospel I preached is not of human origin. I did not receive it from any human source, nor was I taught it; rather I received it by revelation from Jesus Christ" (Galatians 1:11–12 TNIV).

See? Paul's argument is, "My teaching doesn't come from ordinary human beings, my message comes by revelation from Jesus." For him to have thought that this was a biting argument, it is very likely that the opponents *were* taught by human beings not by Jesus. But how could that be threatening to Paul?

Look in your Bible at the paragraphs that follow Galatians 1:11–12. Paul writes about how very, very Jewish he is and then spends paragraphs talking about his relationship with Peter, James, and the other apostles.

Could apostles such as Peter and James be Paul's opponents? No, because Paul would not have made the argument that "my message comes from Jesus" if he was arguing against people who learned at the feet of Jesus; that would play to the opponents' strengths. The likely scenario is that the opponents of Paul are claiming to be students of the disciples. Can you hear how well that backdrop fits the arguments of Paul?

> Those People: Don't believe Paul. Who the heck is Paul? *We*, on the other hand, studied at the feet of those Jewish disciples who studied at the feet of Jesus.
>
> Paul: Don't believe *them*. I don't care who they studied with. I'm more Jewish than they are and my authority comes not from my human teachers but from a heavenly one, just like their teachers', whom, incidentally, I know personally.

That it is the opponents who *start* the fight, by trying to discredit Paul, seems clear from the verses we looked at first, where Paul characterizes them as trying to make the Galatians zealous for *them* in order to alienate Paul (Galatians 4:17). But part of their attempts to discredit Paul also seems visible from the first chapter. Look at these rhetorical questions: "Am I now trying to win the approval of human beings, or of God? Or am I trying to please people? If I were still trying to please people, I would not be a servant of Christ" (Galatians 1:10).

It seems as though it is the opponents who have made it personal.

The Problem

But what is the issue here? What are "Those People" pushing in their teaching that Paul doesn't like? See if you can guess by listening to the epistle:

"Did you receive the Spirit by the works of the Law, or by believing what you heard? Are you so foolish? After beginning with the Spirit, are you trying to finish by human effort?" (Galatians 3:2–3, my paraphrase).

Remember when you were in school and your teacher was sure the class wasn't listening, so she'd repeat things a second time, starting the sentence slow-ly em-pha-sizing each word? That's Paul: "So again I ask, does God give you his Spirit and work miracles among you by the works of the law, or by your believing what you heard?" (Galatians 3:5).

He quizzes the Galatians; what will they answer? Was it by Law or by their faith?

Can you see how Paul's words start to pop off the page? It isn't that he's composing a lecture in which he academically and abstractly compares Law and Faith. Instead, it's a raging argument, with the Gentile Galatians in the middle. "Those People" are saying that they need to keep the Law, and Paul is passionately fighting against that. It's perhaps even clearer a couple of paragraphs later, Paul in full rant mode. Look how many times he crams the phrase "the law" into these few verses – count them:

All who rely on the works of the law are under a curse, as it is written: "Cursed is everyone who does not continue to do everything written in the Book of the Law." Clearly no one who relies on the law is justified before God, because "the righteous will live by faith." The law is not based on faith; on the contrary, it says, "The person who *does* these things will live by them." Christ redeemed us from the curse of the law . . . in order that the blessing given to Abraham might come to the Gentiles through Christ Jesus, so that by faith we might receive the promise of the Spirit (Galatians 3:10–14, emphasis mine).

Did you find them? Five in five verses.

And there is one bit of the Law in particular that Paul returns to over and over. That is part of the initiation rite into Judaism, that mark of the covenant known as circumcision. So, for example, Paul writes: "Those [people] . . . are trying to compel you to be circumcised . . . Not even those who are circumcised keep the law, yet they want you to be circumcised that they may boast about your circumcision in the flesh" (Galatians 6:12–13).

There are clues like this throughout the letter. You do have to be careful when reading them, and not be too sure of your ability to fill in the previous conversation – take your reconstructions with a grain of salt. Use them as hypotheses against which you look again at the letter to see if it makes more sense – to see what pops out, 3D-style.

Having read the whole of the letter, here's an attempt I made of laying out the position of "Those People" in a letter I've called "A Christian letter." Paul's opponents, you see, were not trashing Christianity. I think they may have been trashing Paul, though, and I've over-emphasized this in my reconstructed letter below to make the point. Whatever they thought of Paul, they certainly thought that they were honoring Jesus in what they preached.

Here's the scary thing: when this debate was going on, there was no written New Testament, no gospels as such, just the Old Testament and stories people told you about Jesus. How in the world were you meant to decide which side was right? Feel sorry for the poor Galatians, caught in this high-powered argument between Paul and "Those People".

A Christian letter

The Epistle of "Those People" to the Galatians

1:1 "Those People", entrusted by the pillars of the faith, Jesus' own disciples, with the good news;

1:2 To the believers in Galatia, called to turn from idolatry to the one true God;

1:3 Grace and peace from God our Father and the Lord Jesus Christ.

1:4 We thank God whenever we think of you, being confident that the Lord will keep you walking in the ways he prepared.

Don't Believe Paul

1:5 We beseech you, brothers and sisters, not to be fooled by those who come talking of the gospel but spreading lies. Jesus has not come to destroy the law but to complete it, 1:6 and those, such as Paul, who preach anything else are doing so without the approval of the apostles who sent us, or Jesus who sent them, or God who sent him.

1:7 These teachers are not unknown to us, and they are unstable in all their ways. 1:8 When with Jews, they act as Jews and follow the traditions of the fathers, 1:9 but when with Gentiles, they act as Gentiles and follow the customs of the pagans. 1:10 Such men will do whatever is easiest and whatever gains your approval. But do not be deceived: there are those who seek human approval; they already have all the approval they will ever get. 1:11 Instead, brothers and sisters, seek God's approval by following his will, and God, who sees all things, will reward all things.

The God Who Sent Jesus is Jewish

2:1 For God is a jealous God who sent his son to die for us. He did this, not in order that we may continue in his son but as strangers to himself, but to reconcile us to himself, that we might sit at his table. The Lord Jesus Christ who called you is the Jewish messiah, 2:2 he is God's own answer to Jewish questions and promises. 2:3 But although it is we Jews who are natural heirs to this good news, the bountiful mercy of God is such that he has flung the doors wide open 2:4 that you too can be adopted into the people of God, the Jewish family.

2:5 But this God, whom you now serve in Christ, was not born yesterday. He did not hide himself or his wishes until such time as Jesus appeared. 2:6 No, he spent millennia preparing a people for himself, hinting at his glory and teaching of his character and laws. 2:7 We are not meant to discard all these things as if God has changed his nature overnight. On the contrary, 2:8 the truths that God has revealed in the Scriptures remain as true and valid as ever, though we now see them even more brightly and clearly in the Christ who kept and completed the writings in which he was foretold. 2:9 Has one God withered and another sprouted up? 2:10 No way, José! 2:11 Our God had Jesus always in mind; to those whom he gave the law through Moses he told to expect another prophet like Moses. 2:12 Will the new Moses destroy the work of the first Moses? Will they not both sing from the same song-tablet?

Saying No to the Law is Saying No to God

2:13 And what will God say to us if we say "no" to him? It is not possible to say "yes" to Jesus and "no" to the one who sent him. 2:14 When he gave the Ten Commandments on Mount Sinai, they were not multiple choice. We cannot say, "I love you Lord, and I love your ways" and then say "no" when he bids us "Do not steal." 2:15 Did Jesus keep the commandments or break them? Did Jesus keep kosher or fry bacon? Was Jesus not circumcised? 2:16 If you refuse to follow him in his life, how can you claim to pick up your cross and follow him in his death that you might be raised with him in glory?

2:17 Come out of Egypt and follow the true God! 2:18 If you do not respond in obedience to the Lord, in the commands he gave to his servant Moses, you will have no part in his blessings. 2:19 Embrace the King's commands that you may truly become his subjects and he truly your King.

3:1 Furthermore, brothers and sisters, if you abandon the Law, as some like Paul would have you do, 3:2 you would be constantly sinning and doing what is displeasing to God. For there are only two ways: God's way and sin; there is no neutral ground. 3:3 If God has gone to so much trouble to tell you his way, to make a covenant with people, if God has gone to the trouble of spelling out his holy guidelines for behavior, 3:4 is it really too much to ask for us to learn God's guidelines and keep them and obey his will? 3:5 Come and be part of the covenant with God and help each other not to sin by together keeping the Law!

God's Law and God's Gospel Work Together
3:6 For the Law was not given for its own sake. No, it was always meant to lead to God's ultimate gift to us in his Son. 3:7 If the Law were given for its own sake and Jesus for his own sake, then the one could replace the other, 3:8 but if God is constant and sure from the beginning until now, then they work together. 3:9 The Law leads us to the Christ that it foreshadows 3:10 and it keeps us on the path with him – keeps us from sin. 3:11 Therefore, hear the call of Christ in your hearts and respond with heart and body that you may learn the statutes of God, write them in your body and hearts and obey. 3:12 For the God who created the heavens and the earth loves an obedience with the whole heart but also with all your body, all your soul, and spirit. 3:13 Submit all to him and he will be all in all with you forever.

3:14 Greet all God's people in Christ Jesus; may you know the peace of the Lord as you grow closer and closer inside the clearly declared covenant people of God.

How Christian this teaching sounds. I think if you or I were up against this point of view, we would struggle to know how to reply to it.

Paul composed an excellent one – a reply that perhaps only he could compose. You have it in your Bible: the letter to the Galatians. It has three main parts, each of which is carefully crafted for these particular opponents and this particular congregation. Before he finishes, he will pull rugs out from under his opponents, beat them at their own games several times over, deliberately bore his readers with technical Jewish stuff, liven them up by reminding them of their own exciting experiences, and make a rather embarrassingly rude remark. You may find yourself admiring him, if not liking him a little. I'm pretty sure neither you nor I could have written a better reply. Read the letter to the Galatians for yourself before reading the next chapter. Aloud would be good. In fact, why not find a semi-willing audience who has thirty to forty minutes to spare; read my letter from "Those People" and talk a little bit about the opponents' arguments; then read the letter to the Galatians? Act it out – like two halves of an argument. You and I can talk about it when you get back.

Questions for Discussion or Reflection

1. A big one: I've tried to make the argument of "Those People" as powerful- and Christian-sounding as possible. Before reading Galatians, try thinking through, maybe even sketching on paper, how you might have argued against them in favor of orthodox Christianity. Remember – you can't quote the New Testament, as none of it will have been written yet. You could, though, refer to the words of Jesus. People probably knew quite a bit of Jesus' teaching.

2. Jesus didn't spend a lot of time going to speak to Gentiles, nor did he seem to challenge laws such as circumcision or kosher food laws. What indications do we have in the Gospels that Paul is following Jesus? Would Jesus want us to follow kosher laws and so on today?

3. Many scholars believe that the teachers who caused the trouble at Galatia challenged Paul elsewhere, too, and that the Council of Jerusalem that is written up in Acts 15 was how the larger church replied. Have a look at what was said there. The spirit of the compromise was simple: pagan Gentiles who become Christians do not need to become Jews, but neither may they remain pagan Gentiles: they have to give up pagan practices such as those detailed in Acts 15:29. If the apostles were writing this today, what "pagan" practices might appear in this list instead?

– 5 –

The Genius of Paul's Reply

The Conventions of a Genuine Reply

Paul is not writing about Paul, though we can learn about him through it.

Paul is not writing about us, though the Holy Spirit meant it for us to learn from as well.

First and foremost, Paul was writing about the Galatians. Read the letter with the same mindset as you would listen to one end of a phone conversation. At the other end is a community tempted to fall for an alternative gospel, one that emphasizes obedience to laws given to the Jews.

Paul undermines, refutes, and exceeds everything about the Galatians' new teaching without appearing to do much other than remind them of their good old days together.

Paul's reply first grabs the original readers' attention with something invisible to you. Let me show you.

Turn to the first chapter of the first letter in the New Testament, Romans, and you'll see some formalities at the start. Letter writing in ancient times had conventions and formalities very like our e-mail. There was a FROM: and a TO: line, which was how every letter started. But good writers would fill these in with more than simply names; they would mention those facets of the people's identity that made them the right person to send or receive a particular message. For example, you would expect very different messages from letters beginning in these two ways:

Conrad, New Testament examiner and Study Skills teacher. To Chris, whose intelligence and triumph will be sung by generations of bards.

Conrad, New Testament examiner and Study Skills teacher. To Chris, full of potential, called and chosen by the patient and unconditionally loving God.

In those days, the next thing wouldn't be a SUBJECT line, though. Instead, ancient letters follow FROM: and TO: with GREETING next, usually "peace" although in the case of Christians it's often "grace" or "grace and peace."

After the GREETING comes a THANKS OR PRAISE to the gods. In the case of Jews or Christians, of course, this would be to God in the singular.

Only after these formal steps are complete, will the writer get down to business, usually with words such as "I appeal to you."

In Romans, Paul's FROM: is long – six verses long – probably because it is written to a congregation who don't know him. The TO: and the GREETING are in verse 7. And the THANKS/PRAISE section begins at verse 8.

Turn to the next letter, 1 Corinthians. The FROM: line is in verse 1; the TO: in verse 2; GREETING in verse 3; and THANKS/PRAISE begins in verse 4.

Next, 2 Corinthians. FROM: and TO: in verse 1; GREETING in verse 2; and THANKS/PRAISE in verse 3.

Finally, look at Galatians. The FROM: lines take up verses 1 and 2. See how Paul pads out who he is with information directly relevant to the situation at hand and the content of the letter? He's getting at them right away about human authority. The TO: is just a bare minimum at the end of verse 2 and the GREETING takes verses 3–5. And then . . . Then . . .

See what he does? Or rather what he *doesn't* do? Every ancient reader would have expected another formal section "I am thankful."

Instead, Paul launches directly in with "I am astonished." This is akin to receiving an e-mail like: TO: Chris@yourplace | FROM: Conrad@ mine | SUBJECT: WHAT DID YOU MEAN YESTERDAY WHEN YOU SAID . . . ?

It is not unlike opening a print envelope and instead of finding "Dear Sir or Madam" finding handwritten words. All caps. In red. Crayon.

A letter isn't just a letter; it's a conversation. And *this* conversation is an argument. You may not have noticed it before, but perhaps you can see that the omission of the THANKS will have tipped the Galatians off immediately that Paul is upset and shouting. When you read Galatians through, did you understand what Paul was saying in Galatians 5:12? I won't repeat it here, because you won't believe it's in the Bible until you read it yourself. Paul is angry.

(Here's another thing. Paul didn't intend to write parts of the Bible. Before the New Testament, there aren't really letters in Scripture, so, if he had wanted to write Scripture, he would not have chosen to write in letters. He does not realize that he is writing Scripture. Can you see him letting 5:12 stay in the letter if he had any idea that you and I would be reading it centuries later?)

Paul isn't calmly writing on his theories about religion. He is writing an emotionally charged reply to a situation that has gone wrong. But it is an extremely well-crafted response. As I see it, he confronts his opponents in three main areas. Here's a brief outline of the letter, roughly:

I. Arguments from Paul's life (1:1 – 2:21)
II. Arguments from the Scriptures (3:1–29; see also 4:21 – 5:1)
III. Arguments from their life in the Spirit (4:11 – 5:26)
(Closing: 6:1–18)

The letter doesn't conform to this outline exactly, but these three points form a brilliant reply to the opponents. Paul must first win back credibility for his own authority. He then must defend himself against charges of going against Scripture. But, in these two areas, it's his word against his opponents'. So he closes with a clincher. Once he's got them to see that there are two sides to those arguments, he then hits them between the eyes with something that there cannot be two ways about: their own experience. Paul's trump card is his knowledge of the community in Galatia and his relationship with them. Their new teachers might match his rhetoric, but not his relationship.

Paul and Peter: Not Enemies

The visiting teachers, "Those People," probably made criticism of Paul himself an integral part of the sales pitch for the superiority of their own teachings. Thus Paul is almost required to start out by making himself one of the subjects he discusses. But I maintain that Paul is not really writing about Paul, even when the subject matter is Paul. (Are you still with me?) He writes about their *perception* of him. Are the new visiting teachers in Galatia claiming to be experts in the words and commands of God in the Law? Paul was more zealous than any of them, one of the most advanced Jews of the day (Galatians 1:14).

Even more importantly, Paul turns to the subject of Peter/Cephas before long. Again, I believe that he does this only because the opponents have somehow brought the authority of the Jerusalem apostles into their teaching.

The difference is so very important. The folks who wrote most of the twentieth-century textbooks about Paul seemed sometimes to have assumed that Paul, like them, sat down to write textbooks. It is as if they thought the question Paul was answering was: "What do my ignorant pupils need to know about Christianity?" And if that really had been the question, then, Paul could be read as replying: "First, you need to know that my authority is from God, and that Peter and the Jerusalem apostles are no one special."

But suppose it was a real conversation, and the question was something more like: "Why should we believe you, Paul, when these new teachers studied with Peter, who studied with Jesus?"

Then Paul's reply should be read more like: "Do you think it's impressive that these guys got their message from Peter who got it from Jesus? Well, I got it directly from Jesus. And Peter and the others accepted and affirmed that. Should I shrink from Peter's students when I publicly stood up against Peter himself when he was wrong?"

This is the real meaning of the confrontation story in Galatians 2:11–16. Paul's message is not about Peter's theology and practice being wrong. The real message Paul is putting across is that human teachers like Peter could be wrong.

It doesn't hurt Paul's cause at all that the issue that Peter messed up on was related to Gentiles and the keeping of the Law. And the very clever communicator Paul makes the issue appear even closer; even though the dispute in Antioch was about table fellowship, he calls the opponents there "the circumcision group" (v.12), a name that seems more about the controversy in Galatia than the one in Antioch.

It is not that, in the abstract, Paul hates Peter. Rather, as we've seen, Paul is always conscious of talking on the phone – or rather, I suppose, of being in conversation. He is not dispassionately reciting the facts, he is always applying himself to the particular questions and situations at hand.

"Those People" tried to undermine Paul's authority and his background. Paul, by carefully selecting and recounting details from his own story, not only refutes them, but pulls the rug out from under them. What starts as a defense of his own authority winds up strongly implying the invalidity of *theirs*. And he does it with such subtlety and skill.

45

Old is the New New

One of the reasons that the Gentile Galatians were susceptible to a Christianity that embraced the Jewish Law was the feeling throughout the Roman world that "older is better." It is hard for a person alive today to understand this in the same way. Our preference is always for the "new, improved" version of whatever we can think of. In the ancient world, something new was suspicious; something old was established. So, for example, the first-century Romans tried to make their buildings and statues look like sixth-century BC Greek stuff.

It's not just the pagan world, either. Similar principles held true in Judaism. If you found a verse of the Scriptures difficult, for instance, you might look for another verse in Scripture to explain it, but you would never look forward, only back. The closer you get back to Torah, the first five books of the Bible, the better off you are. And within Torah itself, the closer you get to Creation the better. Thus, Jesus really trumped the Pharisees when they questioned him about divorce in Mark 10:2–9. The passage they quoted from is in Deuteronomy, but Jesus took them back to Genesis – right back to Creation.

The Jewish Torah was revered for being seriously old. The Romans thought that Plato and Socrates were cool because they were old, but Moses lived almost 1,000 years earlier. Romulus and Remus weren't even twin gleams in their foster parent's ancestors' lupine eyes. Enthusiasm was waning for a literal understanding of paganism's hundreds of gods. Judaism had a single, unknowable, non-humanoid God. It was impressive, much more intellectually respectable, and just plain cool.

We even find a class of people called "god-fearers" – people impressed enough with Judaism to want to hang out at the synagogue, but not quite impressed enough to become full Jews and get cut and keep the kosher laws and so on. The Ethiopian eunuch in Acts 8 and Cornelius, the centurion in Acts 10, were in this category, and Paul found this people-group a fertile ground for mission.

Paul's opponents certainly will have made use of Judaism's attractiveness, perhaps by claiming to be more authentically Jewish than he was, sounding very Jewish in their preaching style, and by sharing more of the Law with the Galatians.

But Roman regard for Judaism wasn't *all* positive. Or, rather, regard for Jewish practitioners wasn't that positive. It's like Eastern religions today. If you ask a non-religious person on the street today, "What's the coolest religion?" they're going to say something eastern, like Zen or something. But if you then showed them a Hare Krishna guy, pony-tailed, saffron-robed, tambourine in hand, and dancing, and asked, "What do you think about this guy?" they would probably say something like "That guy? Needs help." It's cool in theory, but in practice? Weird.

Similarly, Judaism in the abstract had attractions, but Jews were not that highly regarded. The Roman philosopher and playwright Seneca wrote in *Moral Letters* that he spent some time as a vegetarian and felt great. But he felt he had to give it up because people would think he was connected to Judaism. For vegetarianism was not common, and everyone knew about Jews not eating pork. It wasn't worth being healthy if people thought you were one of *them*.

Judaism was cool in theory. But Jews? In real life? Not so much.

Here Comes the Jewish Bit

Paul makes stunning use of this ambiguity in his reply. First, as we saw, he is clear that he was advanced in the ancient arts of Judaism beyond most of his age and nobody was more zealous for Judaism (Galatians 1:13–14; cf. 1:23; 2:15–16).

But he also shows this by explaining Scripture symbolically and with allegory. In these sections, Paul might be trying to be deliberately boring. I'm thinking of passages like his discussion of Hagar and Sarah in 4:21 – 5:1. Paul uses a technique that we still use in persuasion today

– in advertising in particular. Some ads can be divided into three parts: a celebrity using the product, looking cool, forms parts 1 and 3. But sandwiched in the middle is something that is deliberately less attractive, sometimes deliberately confusing.

My favorite example is a television shampoo advertisement; maybe you remember it. The model comes on and shakes her head and talks about shine and body and so on. But in the middle of the ad, she says: "Here comes the science bit." And for a few seconds, there's a microscope-like diagram of a hair and words like follicle and enzymes and deoxyribonucleic acid are tossed around. Are you supposed to understand it? No. Why is it there? It's there so that you get the feeling that the people who make the shampoo understand more about it than the pretty model does . . . more about it than you do. The feeling that it sounds scientific and you can't really follow it is precisely what they're trying to achieve. If you could understand it all, it would inspire less confidence than when you are lost.

I believe Paul is doing something like that to his Galatian readers. They have been so impressed with the ultra-Jewishness of their new teachers so he shows them (as well as having told them) that he can do Jewish-style preaching and thinking too – as well or better than his opponents can. And if it feels illogical and difficult for their Gentile minds to follow, well, that's the proof.

Perhaps the most devastating way he plays on these feelings about Judaism, though, comes in Galatians 3. If you or I met some people who were tempted to rely on the Law of Moses, our first impulse would be to insist to them that God has done something new in Christ. Paul is cannier than that with the Galatians. He brings up Abraham, way older than Moses, as the prime example of the man of faith. And then in 3:17, he casually drops the comparison in. Yes, there is the ancient Law of Moses that your teachers are pushing and you think is so cool. But I follow the promise that is 430 years cooler.

The new innovation you've discovered – the Law – cannot nullify the older thing, the Promise.

Paul knows just how to argue with these guys.

Law and Spirit: Not Enemies

When the monk Martin Luther approached Galatians, he did so with a particular set of questions searing his heart and mind: "Why does my religion make me feel so guilty and unworthy? How can a fallible mistake-making creature avoid offending a perfect and holy God?"

It is not that his questions were bad questions. They are excellent questions. They are even questions that God wants to answer and would answer with almost precisely the answers that Luther thought he saw in Galatians. But they are not the Galatian questions that Paul was answering and, as a result, Luther got the answers he was looking for but missed other, beautiful truths.

So when Luther read passages like, "Christ redeemed us from the curse of the law" (Galatians 3:13) and "if you are led by the Spirit, you are not under the law" (Galatians 5:18), it's understandable that he read them as if Paul were teaching that the Law and the Spirit were opposites, enemies headed in different directions.

But the Galatians were not guilt-obsessed monks looking for freedom. They were nearly the opposite: newly converted pagans, seeking to embrace the disciplined life of law that Luther found so oppressive. And because this is not the question that Paul was answering, this is not exactly what his answer means. Paul's answer is not "the Law is evil and the Spirit is good" but rather "the Law was great but the Spirit is even better."

Back in chapter 4, when I composed that letter from the Galatian opponents, I included the notion that if you abandoned the Law, you would be constantly sinning and displeasing God. It is this kind of question that Paul answers by writing "Live by the Spirit, and *you will not* gratify the desires of the flesh" (Galatians 5:16, NIV UK, emphasis mine). Read the section and you'll see: the Law does not lead away from good; the Law leads to the same place that the Spirit leads. It is not that the Galatians must flee from the Law because it will lead them astray, nor does *abandoning* the Law for the Spirit lead them astray. Rather, if they rely on the Spirit they will find that they are *already doing* the kinds of things that the Law wanted them to do, but they are doing so by God's strength rather than by their own.

Imagine you are on an Alpine hiking trail. There are markers for three trails, including the one you're following. You walk along the road and eventually come to a place where a path leaves the road; the path is marked with a little sign that includes the green triangle marker you're following, so you take the path. When the trail forks, you take the branch marked with the green triangle. When the path ends in an open field you go over the stile, shade your eyes, and search until you spy, across the field, a small wooden sign with the green triangle. There is your path.

Keeping the Law is like that. The Christian's life works differently: living with the Spirit is like being on a horse that knows the way home. We are carried along on the right path not because we pull up every so often – saying "Whoa, boy!" – and carefully scan till we find the green triangle. Rather, our job is to stay with the horse, not inadvertently lean one way or the other on the reins, which would divert the horse from its instincts. The horse knows the way home.

So law-free need not mean lawlessness. The law-free gospel leads to the very thing to which the Law was intended to point: righteous, covenant faithfulness.

Is the Law going the wrong way? Is the Law evil? No. We are still to act in accordance with God's ways. Paul does not advocate a faith that remains without works. In chapter 6, Paul exhorts: "let us do good to all" because people reap what they sow (Galatians 6:10,7). And, for Paul, Torah might still have the function of reassuring us we're not leading our horse astray with our inadvertent rein yanking.

Paul's letter is a brilliant answer to the Galatian problem, showing them that the nature of authority has to do with God's calling, not institutional connections, and that doing what God desires involves responding to his Son and keeping in step with his Spirit. Hearing the brilliance of Paul's letter as a reply really put me on the path to liking him better. He is so good at what he does!

What conclusions can we draw out of all this? The first is to realize that there are two questions to answer about this or any biblical text. Two questions. And they must be asked in the right order if we are to make sense of the Bible. Those two questions are the subject of the next chapter.

Questions for Discussion or Reflection

1. If you took some time to prepare your own reply to "Those People," how does yours compare to Paul's?

2. Can you think of examples of times when speakers, maybe even preachers, knew just which subjects to address, and which techniques to use, to reach you? Can you think also of examples where you agreed with the content but found it was conveyed in a way that just didn't connect with you?

3. Does being set free from following the Law mean that Christians have an easier time of it (because of that freedom) or a harder time (because it's sometimes harder to discern what the Spirit wants than read what's written in the Law)?

6

Five Steps, Two Questions, and Some Conclusions

Five Steps

Usually biblical letter writers were writing to people they knew. That meant they could take shortcuts. When Paul wrote in Galatians 4: "you welcomed me as if I were an angel of God," he could count on people having a picture in their head of what went on. We have to think it through and try to imagine what it was like and what it is about that situation that he was trying to bring to his readers' minds. Even noticing that there *are* such gaps in the letter – things we're likely to miss out on – can sometimes take some concentration on our part.

So, I suggest that when you are going to read an epistle, any epistle, you should go through five steps. You can't be completely sure that you know what's going on between the lines of the letter, and there are some things we might never know. But you *can* try to be sensitive to them, and these steps will help with that.

1. Read the letter as a whole, in one sitting if possible.
When you're doing this, ask yourself questions like: What holds this together? What kind of situation might be behind it? Your only goal in this first reading is to embrace the epistle as a whole. (That you notice other things this first time through is a bonus that will help later.)

2. Once you're done with that, skim back through the letter, noting any clues about the situation, copying them down or making a note to look into them further.

Try to look for structural clues not just clues in the content. These are things I've called "texture," such as the omission of the THANKS section in Galatians, or any repetition of phrases.

Look for clues about the author's opponents. Who are they? What in particular has made the author unhappy enough to write? Look for clues about the community to whom the author writes. What is their makeup? What is their relationship to the author?

3. Skim through the text again, this time noticing the arguments that the author makes in his reply.

Try to notice *how* he replies, not just *what* he replies. Note the examples that he uses; these may be big clues about what common ground he shares with the community or the opponents. And, for example, in a letter by Paul, we need to try to notice his Jewish mindset and the Jewish modes of argument he sometimes uses (more about these in coming chapters).

4. Read the epistle as a whole again, now that you're beginning to understand it and its background. This time, don't read it seeking clues. (But keep a notebook at the ready to jot any down . . . for you'll usually find many more when you're no longer trying.) Instead, this time, listen to it speaking to that situation you'll have identified.

5. Now, and only now, ask yourself these two questions, and ask them in this order: What *did* it mean? What *does* it mean?

The Two Questions

I have no doubt that God could have selected someone with good handwriting and dictated Scripture to them. If he had done this, if the Bible had been written directly from God to you and me, then perhaps we could dispense with some of these procedures in our reading. Still, though, you'd have to guess that some of what was in Scripture was aimed at *my* failings, and therefore would be unnecessary for you.

Instead, God chose to provide this part of Scripture by giving us documents that grew out of problems and responses in first-century communities. Honoring his choice means taking those situations seriously. Understanding the documents we have involves understanding the problems and how these letters respond to them.

In many ways, this is the most important thing that I could teach you from this book. Ask what the text *meant* in its original historical context before you ask what it *means* for today. What it meant – what God used it to accomplish then – is not always going to be same as what it means – what God intends for today. But the *then* is likely to inform our decisions about the *now*.

So, you need to start with the first question. What *did* it mean? What is the cumulative effect of the arguments? What did Paul (or Peter or James or whoever the author was) want to convince that particular community to do? Why?

And then you can ask yourself the other question: What *does* it mean? What does it mean to us in the twenty-first century and how do we apply it?

Hermeneutics and Old Testament specialist Richard Briggs loves to tell students that eating meals in restaurants is forbidden by the New Testament. Some probably expect him to show a verse about not being extravagant, being good stewards of your money, and so on. Instead he pulls out 1 Corinthians 11:34, "if anyone is hungry, let him eat at home" (ESV). To me, this demonstrates the idea that until you ask the question "What *did* it mean?" it's very easy to get the wrong answer to the question "What *does* it mean?"

If you're interested, figuring out what Paul was actually saying there is frequently called *exegesis*, while figuring out what that all might mean for today might be called *interpretation* or *application* depending on how theoretical or practical it is. And figuring out what sort of principles help us get to the right answer and might prevent us making the same mistake with other passages is the science of *hermeneutics*.

An expert, of course, would find more nuances and overlap than we can be concerned about here. In the final analysis perhaps they are harmony and melody of the same song rather than separate songs. But what matters is carefully, respectfully, and rightly handling the word of God so that we receive the messages that God has gone to lots of trouble to get in there.

Some Conclusions

So here's what we did with Galatians: we assessed the situation which, according to clues scattered through the six chapters of the letter, concerns someone, perhaps with impressive credentials, preaching a sort of "gospel of works" butting in on the hospitable and impressionable community that Paul started up.

After an overview of the situation, we looked at Paul's arguments. He draws heavily on his experiences with the so-called Jerusalem pillars, and then on the Abraham traditions in the Old Testament, although ultimately he comes back to arguments that are based on his readers'/hearers' experiences and contrasts that make sense to them: sons versus slaves, life in the Spirit versus the sinful nature.

Like a lioness protecting her cubs, Paul roars courageously back at the interlopers who are trying to turn the enthusiastic new Gentile believers into obedient little Jewish clones. I imagine the males in his audience are gratefully amused at his sarcastic and outrageous suggestion about emasculation for those teachers who are telling them they must undergo painful surgery before they can truly join God's community (Galatians 5:12).

But it's not all bluster, anger, and outrage. Paul shows deep insight in ways we might not expect from someone who had formerly been so indoctrinated in the religious path of the Pharisees. For instance, who could have expected anyone at this stage in the community's short history to be already thinking about the differences between spiritual authority and churchly institutional authority? His ministry was recognized by, not authorized by, Peter and James and those reputed to be pillars. Then again, perhaps the nature of Jesus' authority did that for reflective thinkers like Paul.

Paul also shows great insights into the message underlying Jesus' own attitude toward the Law of Moses. The Lord seemed to be at once willing to flout the Law, while also talking about it with great respect and treating it as the treasure along the lines of Psalm 119. And Paul's attitude might be summed up well by paraphrasing one of Jesus' more enigmatic teachings: people were not created for the sake of the Law, but the Law for people (see, for instance, Mark 2:27; 10:5). The idea that relationship with God is a great and free gift we cannot earn by our good religious behavior is at the heart of both their efforts. You can imagine Paul watching the initial response of the Galatians hinted at in this letter and marveling with Jesus, "I have not found such great faith even in Israel." Paul's opponents haven't really gotten to grips with Jesus' revolutionary thinking. Somehow, Paul has.

And Paul further shows insight in understanding what will defeat this party of "Judaizers" and great skill in pulling it off. He understands how to do this because he has truly listened. He appreciates the thinking and the hopes of his people in Galatia because he has attended to them. And he takes pains to appreciate and understand the strong and weak points of his opponents' ways of thinking too, so that he can reply to their system forcefully and effectively. The early section on his relationship with the "pillars" of the Jerusalem church, for instance, or his engagement with the Old Testament Scriptures and the idea of "old is good" all show him engaging with the opponents on their own ground. But, of course, the master-stroke is bringing it all back to the Galatian believers' own experiences, which just happen to be experiences shared with their first Christian teacher, Paul.

It's time to answer our twin questions: What did it mean? What does it mean?

What it meant for the Galatians in the first century is by now pretty clear to you. Get rid of those guys! Don't be circumcised; rely on grace, faith, and promise. Once you understand the letter as a whole, you find summaries pop out at you, as with these sections of three verses each:

All of you who were baptized into Christ have clothed yourself with Christ. There is neither Jew nor Gentile, neither slave nor free, nor is there male and female, for you are all one in Christ Jesus. If you belong to Christ, then you are Abraham's seed, and heirs according to the promise (3:27–29).

You who are trying to be justified by the law have been alienated from Christ; you have fallen away from grace. For through the Spirit we eagerly await by faith the righteousness for which we hope. For in Christ Jesus neither circumcision nor uncircumcision has any value. The only thing that counts is faith expressing itself through love (5:4–6).

That's what it meant. What does it mean for us today?

To some extent that will depend on the details of each of our own particular situations. But it certainly says something to us about access to the community of God's people and membership in it – how to get in and how to stay in.

For all Christians, Galatians has a message of freedom. We are free *from* certain things, such as from having to struggle to become a part of God's community. It is a gift, not something we have to accomplish. In the same way, we're free from having to struggle to *stay* in God's community. We are free from labels such as "slave," "free," "handicapped," or whatever. Galatians is for us about God loving us no matter who or what we were in the world's eyes. And for some of us it's also important to hear that we're free from a reliance on ritual, a slavery to things that are either human-made or made-for-humans.

But Galatians is not only about what we are free *from*, it's also about what we are free *to*. There's a formulation of this that Luther loved – I believe he got it from Augustine: "Love God and do as you then please." You can hear Galatians 5:16 behind that provocative wording: "So I say, walk by the Spirit, and you will not gratify the desires of the flesh." We are free to love God and do as we then please.

As we hinted at the end of the previous chapter, Paul is clear that we are still to do good, to serve each other (Galatians 6:1–10). But this doing good is not a legislated rule of admittance. It is a *response*. It's not what we *have to do* in order to become a Christian or stay a Christian. It is the *expression* of Christianity, not the essence of Christianity.

"Neither circumcision nor uncircumcision means anything; what counts is the new creation" (Galatians 6:15).

Love God – that's the crucial bit – and do as you then please. Because if you truly love God, then doing what you please will involve doing loving-God things.

The skill of Paul can be seen in what looks at first to be a mere dollop of nostalgia back in 4:14–15: "and even though my illness was a trial to you, you did not treat me with contempt or scorn. Instead, you welcomed me as if I were an angel of God, as if I were Christ Jesus himself. Where, then, is your blessing of me now? I can testify that, if you could have done so, you would have torn out your eyes and given them to me." How far from the law of "an eye for an eye" (Exodus 21:23–5; cf. Matthew 5:38) is their care for Paul and how much more like God in Christ. He is not just reminding them of what they were. This is no idle longing for the past – this is what he wants them to be like again.

Isn't Paul good? Skillful and smart and surgical in his strikes (not to mention recommendations). And, of course, he's right. This is the side you'd want to be on, isn't it? Our faith is about being in relationship with Christ through the Holy Spirit, rather than adhering to rules and regulations. But how well he sees it and argues for it – before the New Testament was written to refer to!

And that is the book of Galatians. In the next chapter, we'll start a new section in which we will look at another letter. From clues there, you'll learn about an explosive situation at the church in Corinth. If you want to investigate for yourself, you could read the letter of 1 Corinthians, looking for clues about their relationship with Paul. Also ask yourself what the Corinthians were like as a people. And, perhaps most fun of all, can you spot the places throughout the letter where Paul is throwing their own quotations back at them?

Questions for Discussion or Reflection

1. I gave a somewhat humorous example of 1 Corinthians 11:34, "if anyone is hungry, let him eat at home" (ESV), as if it were about not eating at restaurants. Are there verses that you held on to once but came to realize didn't say what you thought they did?

2. Galatians is about freedom; and we are free from certain things and free to do others. How do you think your own faith makes you "free from" and "free to"?

3. As I directed you in the final paragraph of this chapter, skim through 1 Corinthians and see if you can find clues about their relationship with Paul and even occasions where Paul quotes things that the Corinthians have said.

PART III:

Tighten Up –
1 Corinthians

7

Paul and the Corinthians

Orientation Needed

Moving into a new neighborhood; opening to the first page of a novel; walking into the building on the first day at a new job; seeing the credits fade away at the start of a film – you don't make progress until you know the lay of the land. Orienting yourself is crucial.

We saw with Galatians that understanding what went on before Paul wrote the letter helped us immensely in understanding what he intended to teach in reply to the people then and in understanding what the book might be saying to us today.

It's worth seeing if the same might be true about our next letter, 1 Corinthians. As you can imagine, I probably wouldn't have selected this letter to do next if I didn't think that were true!

So: if finding out what went on before the letter is important to gaining a true understanding of what the letter is saying, then, paradoxically, the wisest path to the message of the letter might be to put the message to one side at first and concentrate on sleuthing – unearthing clues about the background. What happened in Corinth? There are clues scattered over the letter like power-ups on a computer game roadway. Let's see if we can maneuver right into them . . . ka-zzzzing!

Clues from the Outset

If you're watching out for clues, you don't have to venture far into 1 Corinthians before you'll spot something glimmering at you in a corner. What made Paul write this letter? Verse 11 of the very first chapter says: "some from Chloe's household have informed me." Paul has heard reports from some people about the Corinthians' recent behavior – quarrels and things – and these have motivated him to write.

Reading around this verse tells you that they quarreled because Paul was not the only leader that they championed. Some claimed to follow him, but others claimed to follow Apollos, others Cephas/Peter, and still others Christ. Wait; aren't people who follow Paul also followers of Christ? Shh. You're moving too fast. At the moment, we're only looking for clues. At some point we'll need to figure out who Apollos was too. Was he there in Corinth? Was Peter? As far as we know, Christ never went there in the flesh. Maybe the other two opposed Paul's teaching just as the visitors to Galatia opposed Paul? Whoa. We'll come back to this.

Something peculiar is going on in 1:14–17. From that passage, it seems safe to infer that Paul had been in Corinth before so knew the community personally. He baptized at least some of the people in the Corinthian church (presumably having also converted them). But look at all the things he is at pains to deny in this passage. Odd things to deny, aren't they? Think of your minister for a minute. Can you imagine him or her standing up in front of your congregation and saying: "I'm glad I didn't baptize any of you"? Yet Paul says, "I thank God that I did not baptize any of you except . . ." (1:14) and "Christ did not send me to baptize, but to preach . . . not with wisdom and eloquence" (1:17). We're at the clue-collecting stage for now, but we are surely going to have to answer this question: why would Paul write as though baptizing people were bad and as though wisdom and eloquence were bad things? Does he have a low opinion of baptism? Or is there something in the practice or beliefs of the Corinthians that make him write this way?

At this stage, the first things you find out will feel like they're raising more questions for you than giving answers. Sort of like when you are orienting yourself with a new job. But don't give up! You may have more questions now than before, but now they're the *right* questions. We see now that we have some possible opponents for Paul and we also detect his strange reticence to talk about his own ministry. As we keep finding clues, these things will make more and more sense.

Another big clue about the Corinthians themselves comes in verse 26 of chapter 1: "Think of what you were when you were called. Not many of you were wise by human standards; not many were influential; not many were of noble birth." But was Paul there at their first "calling"? Did he found that community, as we know he did the Galatian one?

Chapter 2:1–5 is the first place that Paul specifically writes about his time in Corinth. The people that he mentions he baptized could, theoretically, have traveled to Paul when he converted them and baptized them, but Paul in 2:1 makes it clear that he was the one who traveled: "when I came to you." In this passage we again get the disclaimers about wisdom and eloquence. He came and he preached, without wisdom or eloquence, resolving to know nothing except Christ crucified. Here in chapter 2, the repetition of the phrase "human wisdom" (2:1,5) and the contrast between "human wisdom" and "God's power" (2:5) reinforce what is argued throughout these early chapters. Despite the fact that "not many of [the Corinthians] were wise by human standards" (1:26), there is something about the Corinthians that makes Paul emphasize a negative attitude toward human wisdom when he writes to them. They were not wise, and so when Paul was with them, he gave them "milk" not "solid food," because they weren't ready for it (3:2). In chapter 3, this theme is then woven together with that of following particular leaders. More about these themes later.

When these passages are combined with 4:15, "in Christ Jesus I became your father through the gospel" and 9:1–2, "are you not the result of my work in the Lord?" and "you are the seal of my apostleship in the Lord," it becomes a safe inference that Paul not only visited Corinth, but also founded the church there.

So let's take stock of what we've learned through these various clues: Paul went to Corinth and preached the gospel and people responded and became Christians. Then, at some point, presumably, Paul moved on (since he's now writing them a letter from somewhere else). At another point – perhaps much later – people from Chloe's household visited Paul and informed him about the situation there. And, as a result, Paul started writing the letter we call 1 Corinthians. Oh, and somehow, some of the Corinthians started following Peter and Apollos rather than Paul. How did that happen? And how will Paul try to win them back?

After Paul Left

What went on in Corinth between Paul's leaving them and Chloe's people reporting to him?

Well, all sort of situations seem to have arisen internally as a result of the Corinthians trying to live day-by-day as Christians in Corinth or, rather, in their case, as Corinthians who are also Christians. We'll look at these below when we talk about some of the issues Paul feels he has to write about, ranging from lawsuits to the Lord's Supper.

If Paul was the first Christian preacher they heard, but now some of the Corinthians are claiming to follow others, is it because those others have been there and, like the opponents in Galatia, were stealing Paul's followers away from him? Could 1 Corinthians have been written to help those who said "I follow Paul" argue against the others who say "I follow Apollos" and "I follow Peter"?

It does seem as though Apollos visited Corinth. Look at the clue in 3:6, "I planted the seed, Apollos watered it;" the obvious understanding is that Paul began the church and Apollos nurtured its growth. But, wow: such *positive* language compared to anything Paul said about the Galatian opponents, which is more like "I planted, they revved up a chainsaw." Further, at the end of the letter, Paul writes, "Now about our brother Apollos: I strongly urged him to go to you with the brothers. He was quite unwilling to go now, but he will go when he has the opportunity" (1 Corinthians 16:12). This is both an important clue about the intervening events – it's likely that Apollos visited Corinth, but also clear that he's not there now – and also about Paul's attitude toward Apollos. Again, think back to all you learned about Galatians; can you imagine Paul urging the Galatians' visiting lecturers to go back to teach them some more? He's more likely to run 'em the other way. With a shotgun.

This timetable of events is borne out if we "cheat" and have a look at Paul's travels as reported outside the letter, in the book of Acts. There we can read about Paul's arrival and mission work in Corinth and how he stayed there for a year and a half before sailing off to Syria (Acts 18:1–18). The text of Acts even tells us about Apollos: first, how believers met him in Ephesus and then how he traveled on to Corinth in the region of Achaia after Paul had left and was in Ephesus (Acts 18:24 – 19:1). The clues in the letter easily line up with the narrative in Acts.

We have fewer clues about whether Peter/Cephas visited. Most commentators think not, but what I read in 1 Corinthians 9:4–6 (and the rest of the section all the way to verse 18) makes me think that the people in Corinth may indeed have been trying to compare the practices of Peter and Paul, as if both were familiar to them.

In any case, Paul is against the divisions in the church – the separation of the community into cliques claiming different leaders, but the thrust of chapter 3:4–9 ("We are co-workers in God's service; you are God's field" [v.9]) is that he does not see the leaders themselves as opponents, but as working together for the same end (and, in chapter 9, within their rights even where their practices diverge from his own).

And *this*, probably, explains why it is that a church leader would be glad that he didn't baptize many people. He is not defending the "I follow Paul" clique nor wishing it to grow – he celebrates not having given them cause to claim him over another. He is against the divisions themselves, not against Cephas and Apollos (and Christ). So we don't have the same sort of triangle of Paul, the readers, and the bad-guy teachers as we had in Galatians.

Other Recent Contact

Now if you've read the letter looking for clues, I hope you noticed that Paul does not get all of his information about current events from "Chloe's people." Instead, there seems to have been a previous correspondence. Did you see 1 Corinthians 5:9? "I wrote to you in my letter not to associate with sexually immoral people." Since he here explains the advice that he says he gave there, he cannot be talking about 1 Corinthians – it is not "earlier in this letter," it must be "in my previous letter." That means, of course, that 1 Corinthians is not, technically, *first* Corinthians. But for ease of reference with the rest of the world, let's continue to call it that. We can call the letter referred to in 5:9 Zero Corinthians.

He wrote to them and they wrote back. Hopefully you noticed the further clue that chapter 7 begins with: "Now for the matters you wrote about." Apparently the Corinthians wrote a letter to Paul but we no longer have it. One of the subjects in it will have concerned the theme of this chapter: marriage and singleness.

Here's something I'll bet you didn't notice though. Ready? See the short phrase at the beginning of 7:1 "Now for the matters you wrote about . . ."? Good.

Turn to 8:1: "Now about food sacrificed to idols . . ."

Turn to 12:1: "Now about the gifts of the Spirit . . ."

15:1: "Now, brothers and sisters, I want to remind you of . . ."

16:1: "Now about the collection . . ."

And finally, turn to 16:12: "Now about our brother Apollos . . ."

See where I'm going with this? Maybe Paul deals with the reports from Chloe's people in chapters 1 – 6. Then, in chapters 7 – 16, Paul turns to the letter from the Corinthians, and deals with the matters that they brought up, one at a time. "Now – about the next thing in your letter."

There's just one other main contact source to mention: we were introduced to Chloe's household in chapter 1; chapter 16 makes clear that there was another group of people who visited Paul from Corinth, "I was glad when Stephanas, Fortunatus and Achaicus arrived" (16:17). Their presence ripples forward in the letter too, and we see a brief mention of them in parentheses in 1:16, in circumstances that make us wonder whether Stephanas was proof-reading Paul's letter. I can just imagine the conversation:

Paul: "I didn't baptize anyone but Crispus and Gaius."
Stephanas: "Uh, Paul, you baptized me and my household too, remember?"
Paul, hitting forehead with the heel of his palm: "Oh, duh, all right, the household of Stephanas. Other than that I don't remember."

So, you see, we can figure out quite a bit from the clues in the letter. Paul went to Corinth and preached, apparently deliberately choosing to avoid sounding like some eloquent teacher. After he left, other teachers – such as Apollos – came on the scene and the Corinthians began taking sides. Presumably, they also started compromising, and their morality occasioned a letter from Paul warning them about it. They wrote back to Paul with a letter that appears to have covered a range of subjects, including relationships and marriage. In our "1" Corinthians, Paul responds to that letter, to reports from Chloe's household, and perhaps to reports from Stephanas' household as well.

Okay, now here's something you (and my editor) don't want to hear: not all of this information is going to be equally enlightening in understanding the letter. I don't mean not relevant in *applying* the letter, I mean in *understanding*. Some of it will and some of it won't. The thing is, you don't know what will be useful and helpful ahead of time. But while not all of it is useful, if it's in Scripture and you believe what I believe, then all of it is from God. So if I need to learn a little more than I'm going to use in order to try to ensure I've learned enough to understand better, well, that seems a reasonable trade-off. Most people who write or speak to you about the Bible have learned more than they need to know or need to communicate. They then streamline, and only tell you the *relevant* things that they've learned. But I'm not just teaching you about the kernel of 1 Corinthians, I'm teaching you how to get at that kernel. It's like the more that you know about everything that can go wrong with an old John Deere tractor's engine, the more easily you can diagnose and deal with the one or two things that actually have.

So don't just learn about what you think can help you. Learn about what is true, learn about what is from God, and you'll find the tasks of understanding and applying will go that much easier when you get to them.

Our next task will be identifying the Corinthians' problems – where they especially needed the truth of God to be applied to their lives. And – poor Paul – Corinth had no shortage of these. Will he be up to the task?

Questions for Discussion or Reflection

1. In this chapter I have asked you again to be interested in the truth behind the book without considering whether you'll be able to apply it directly to your life or not. Think/discuss whether you believe it's an important thing to do on your own as well.

2. The Corinthians, I've suggested, revered their leaders too much, claiming them as gurus. Does the church do this today? Have you ever found yourself doing this with a church leader or writer?

3. As we've seen, Paul wrote telling the Corinthians that he was glad he didn't baptize many of them – but there was a specific reason he said that. Have you got any humorous stories of things you have said or advised that don't make sense out of context?

8

Already You Are Kings!

The Many Issues

We've talked about the way that the Corinthians' everyday lives threw up issues, some of which caused them to act in ways that took them away from God rather than toward him.

We've already mentioned the somewhat curious business of the "I follow X" and "I follow Y" divisions at Corinth and how it seems that it was the followers who might have been at war with each other rather than the leaders in this case. This division issue is, in the first few chapters of 1 Corinthians, constantly intertwined with the business of wisdom and foolishness.

If you think about it, this makes sense. Part of the Greek culture in which Corinth was soaked involved lining yourself up with a philosophical school and a teacher, or sophist, who became your guru and hero. In Greece, the rivalries between the adherents of such systems were commonplace. Listen to the relentless cynicism of Dio Chrysostom who, maybe forty years after Paul, wrote of another visitor to Corinth, who found in the city squares "crowds of wretched sophists around Poseidon's temple shouting and reviling one another, and their disciples, as they were called, fighting with one another, many writers reading aloud their stupid works . . . fortune-tellers interpreting fortunes, lawyers innumerable perverting judgment, and peddlers, not a few, peddling whatever they happened to have" (Discourses, 8:9).

We will find, in many ways, the Corinthian Christians acted more like people who were trying to do Christianity in a Corinthian way than they were like people trying to be Corinthians in a Christian way. It is not, probably, that there was anything about Apollos and Paul themselves that caused the divisions. Rather, these people were used to aligning themselves with one teacher, and seeing those who lined up with another as adversaries.

They certainly acted like Corinthians when it came to sexual matters. Paul had to write to them about these things in his "previous" letter (5:9) and does so again here. There was a temple to Aphrodite in Corinth that, according to ancient writers, was said to be the workplace of a thousand cultic prostitutes. But that temple had been destroyed more than a hundred years before Paul visited Corinth. Yet the reputation remained. Commentators love to mention that Corinth was so well known for its loose morals that people used the expression "corinthian girl" about a female of dubious morality wherever she was from, in the way that we use the term "french fries" for potato snacks of a certain shape whether they were prepared in Paris or Indiana.

Another example is the lawsuits, a topic Paul dealt with in chapter 6. The excerpt from Dio above mentioned lawyers perverting justice and Corinth was, indeed, a litigious place. The Christians there acted no differently. Paul's rebuke is scathing: "The very fact that you have lawsuits among you means you have been completely defeated already. Why not rather be wronged?" (1 Corinthians 6:7).

We mentioned the issue of marriage that comes up in chapter 7, but chapter 8 introduces a topic that is strange to modern ears: "Now about food sacrificed to idols . . ." (8:1). Discussed in 8:1–13, Paul then appears to digress from the matter for a while before returning to the theme in 10:14 – 11:1. Let me explain the cluster of issues: meals were of great significance throughout the different cultures of the ancient world. Western commentators often present it as if the ancients were unusual in regarding "table fellowship" as charged with significance. But that's wrong. It is *we* who are the odd ones in the way that we generally *remove* significance from mealtimes.

Think of the first time you went to have dinner at someone's house as a boyfriend or girlfriend and you begin to taste the social significance that all mealtimes tend to have outside our hurried and individualistic culture. Who you eat with, and how, is critically important to everyone except us. Jesus demonstrated acceptance of the down-and-outs of society by eating with them. So, in Corinth, the question of whether you were inviting pagan deities to be your accepted and close friends was a serious one. Some Corinthian Christians, apparently, continued to eat at social functions at their local temples when invited; they knew now that there weren't really gods behind these idols, that it was all just superstition that couldn't affect them now that they were in Christ. But other Corinthian Christians seem to have found this offensive. I guess the closest analogy might be finding out that a male church elder had dinner at a topless lap-dancing club the night before. "I just like the food there," he says. "I wasn't looking at the women." Some of the Corinthians would have approved of this elder's spiritual flaunting of what other, "weaker" Christians might think of as rules.

In chapters 10 to 14, Paul deals with various matters relating to church practice in Corinth. The ones that usually garner the most attention are spiritual gifts and their practice and the matter of women's roles, but there is also a section on the Lord's Supper that is quite remarkable and unlike any other passage in Paul's letters. All in all, though, their worship services seem as though they must have been chaotic. Paul writes: "your meetings do more harm than good" (11:17).

Right smack in the middle of a discussion of their behavior at their worship services is 1 Corinthians 13, the love chapter. Paul is not talking about weddings in the churches, but the use of spiritual gifts. And that's how the chapter starts: "If I speak in the tongues of men or of angels, but do not have love, I am only [noise]" (13:1). It fits well into its context in the book. While Paul didn't write this passage specifically about marital love, it is not out of place read at weddings, as long as we never believe that our spouse or our families are the *only* people to whom we should act in this self-giving way.

There is one more big issue in the letter: the hope of a future resurrection (1 Corinthians 15). If you read carefully, it looks as though the Corinthians do not doubt that Christ rose from the dead, for Paul seems to refer to this as common ground rather than arguing it at length. What they seem to doubt is that there is a future resurrection for them. Their souls are eternal and safe in Christ and they don't seem to think that they need anything like a future bodily resurrection.

Chapter 16 closes out with two less consequential matters that Paul appears to be answering from their letter to him: first, he clarifies instructions about a collection of funds that he is helping supervise in order to support the Jerusalem church (16:1–4). This is followed by information about travel plans: his own, Timothy's, Apollos', and Stephanas' people. And all that remains after that are fairly standard closing greetings.

Symptoms and Disease

One of the things that I long for you to be able to do is observe what's there in Scripture and roll it around in your mind, looking at it in different ways to see if you can spot any patterns. So, does anything strike you about this range of issues?

Something that occurred to scholars back in the twentieth century is that one of the issues is different from all the others. So many of the matters Paul wrote about concerned proper Christian practice and behavior. Only one, the resurrection, seems purely about an idea, a Christian belief. Many academics, especially ones who themselves think that ideas are most important, have explored the hypothesis that the Corinthians' attitude toward the resurrection is at the root of all their other problems; the disease of which things like their bad behavior are symptoms. Let me explain how this might be.

The best guess about the Corinthians' beliefs is that they were rooted in the Greek philosophy that they inherited. They are likely to have believed that whatever is physical is limiting and bad, whereas the non-physical is the truer, purer reality. This is not what either Christianity or Judaism teach, exactly.

For Christians and Jews, the physical universe is not inherently evil but a good creation of God, although it has been corrupted in the Fall. And, for us, the soul or psyche of a person is not pristine and unfallen; on the contrary, our decision-making facilities are just as prone to sin.

Anyway, the Corinthians may have been stuck in their Greek mindset and assumed, therefore, that what Christianity did was make you a new, more spiritual person inside. They may have believed that that work was done at conversion or baptism so now they were new, eternal, saved creatures so didn't need to wait for something later. "A physical resurrection? Why in the world would anyone want *that*? Surely, the point is to free one's eternal soul from the lumbering, encumbering, limiting matter!" they would have said.

That's the hypothesis, anyway. And, certainly, elements of this kind of thinking can be read back in a way that throws new light on some of the other issues. For instance, their casual attitude toward sexual behavior would make sense if they believed that the spirit or soul is eternal and important, but the husk of physical body doesn't really count for anything. The saying of the Corinthians', which Paul quotes back to them, "Food for the stomach and the stomach for food" (6:13), is indicative of this kind of attitude. (Although the stomach was not the only bit of their anatomy they were thinking this applied to.) Their attitude was: "Let the physical body do whatever it wants because it is irrelevant to our own spiritual self."

Tracing the implications of the faulty view of resurrection is helpful. Ultimately, though, it doesn't really explain enough of the issues in the book to sustain the hypothesis that it is the underlying theme of the *whole* letter. But I do think there is an important principle here: their views about resurrection stem from forcing Christianity into their perspective as Corinthians, trying to mold Christianity around the thinking and living they already had.

Another hypothesis about the underlying core of the book goes back to the first few chapters rather than the end. The Corinthian church is divided. Perhaps it is their divisiveness and lack of community that is the root cause of all their problems.

A clear example of how this problem underlies another is in the case of the use of spiritual gifts in the Corinthians' worship services. The more that you read chapters 12 and 14, the more clear it becomes why chapter 13, about love, is in the middle. To get to the solution of the Corinthian problem, they don't need to learn more about the gifts, they need to learn more about how the gifts should be used for building each other up. The surface subject may be "speaking in tongues" but the real problem and its solution lies not in practicing the gift of tongues, but in practicing the discipline of doing what is best for other people.

What Paul is teaching them is that spiritual maturity is not measured best by how much and how often you "share" your spiritual gift with others or force it on them. True spiritual maturity is better measured by the correct use of a gift, such as prophecy accompanied by interpretation. The question is not how hard have you worked or how frequently have you spoken or spoken in tongues? The real question is how encouraged and built-up is the community because of your service, whether silent or vocal?

That they don't care enough about others is clear throughout the letter, but it gains even more explanatory power if you turn the emphasis around. The reason that they didn't care enough about other people is, I believe, because the community was self-centered and self-important. This is probably a better way of putting it than saying that they didn't care about others, although, obviously, the two go hand in hand.

Not unlike our own Western culture in many ways, Corinthian culture was a "me-first" culture, a "looking out for number one," a "because I'm worth it" culture. And it is this, I believe, that is the disease that explains the various symptoms we read about in 1 Corinthians.

Their unbridled conceit is probably the reason that Paul reminds them in 1:26–29 that not many of them were wise or influential, and that God chose the weak things, the lowly and despised, so that no one can boast. He attacks their conceit in a different way in 4:7–13, dripping with sarcasm in verse 8 especially: "Oh, you already *have* everything you need; already you've become *rich*. Already you've been crowned kings and queens – but if so, you've done it without us! How I wish you really *had* become kings and queens that we might reign along with you" (my paraphrase).

In 5:1–2,6, we see that they're not only doing the wrong things but actually boasting about their "liberated" morality. They think they're cool. The lawsuits in chapter 6 show that they are also looking out for number one. At least part of their problem with the Lord's Supper in chapter 11 is that they eat and drink without waiting for each other – with a "no one matters but me" attitude. And their problem with spiritual gifts, as we've seen, is a relational problem: "I want more gifts and more power and my gift is the best and should be used and heard in the meetings."

So when the Corinthians say "I follow Paul" and "I follow Apollos," is that an exception to their self-centeredness? Probably not. Again, when you read the passages closely, the picture is not that of humble following, but of asserting credentials. It's as if the important word in "I follow Christ" was not *Christ* or *follow* but *I*. There is a certain kind of person who wears the T-shirt from a band not primarily because they like the band, but because they want you to know that they're the kind of person who likes the band. There's a kind of person that buys Apple gear not because it's better but because they think they'll look cooler. *That's* the Corinthians.

These are a people who think that they've arrived, spiritually. Already they have everything they could want. Who needs a resurrection? And who needs other people, and rules and regulations that keep putting the emphasis on the physical stuff that is of lesser importance?

My apologies if you've felt we've been trekking uphill in this chapter. But you'll find that the scenic view was worth the climb. So here's the pay-off: dip into 1 Corinthians in one or two places at random and read for ten or twelve verses each and watch how your new knowledge of their "superiority complex" can bring most passages back to life, even suggesting the tone and attitude you should use to read them.

Now, how can you get through to people who think they've already *arrived*, how do you argue with people who think that they know everything?

Get ready to watch Paul and learn.

Questions for Discussion or Reflection

1. How would you have gone about the task of writing a reply to the Corinthians? Without looking at the letter, try your hand at giving your advice on one or two of the matters needing attention.

2. We've looked at the idea that various different-looking symptoms can be caused by one underlying disease. Without criticizing others, or getting too personal, can you identify some symptoms in, say, your attitude toward church, that are actually caused by something deeper?

3. The Corinthians felt themselves superior. Can feelings of inferiority cause problems too, or should Christians be extra humble? How can we learn to find a balance?

9

How to Argue with a Corinthian

Parallel Argument Style

Before really getting to the heart of the arguments that Paul uses deliberately with the Corinthians, I can't resist showing you an argument style that I believe Paul uses unconsciously. There are such good examples of it in 1 Corinthians.

You know how a typical argument works. It's a process that starts with something basic and then builds up gradually, step-by-step, taking us to a logical conclusion. But when Paul gets excited he frequently lapses into a more Jewish mode of arguing, which is more like a set of side-by-side arguments rather than a single step-by-step argument.

This can sometimes lead to confusion on our part when we try to interpret it all the way through, because often the only thing that the parallel arguments are meant to have in common is the conclusion.

An example is 1 Corinthians 6:12–20. This passage confused the daylights out of me once. I was writing something about Ephesians 1:22–3 and the way it uses the analogy of Christ being the head and us Christians making up his body. I knew that similar imagery is splattered all over 1 Corinthians, so I came to chapter 6 with a particular question in mind: What is the relationship of our bodies to the Trinity?

Having read this far you'll know the trouble I was in for, asking a question of Paul's letter that was not the question Paul was answering.

I found a relevant nugget in 6:15: "Do you not know that your bodies are members of Christ himself?" That fit with my Ephesians passage nicely. Our bodies are parts of Christ.

But then at the end of the paragraph I discovered this: "Do you not know that your bodies are temples of the Holy Spirit . . .?" (6:19) Wait . . . what does *that* imply about the Trinity? If, step one, our bodies are bits of Christ, but, step two, each of them is a temple of the Holy Spirit then . . . what? I reeled.

I never finished that study. I was making two basic errors. First, I was *using* the text rather than listening to it, treating it as my servant rather than my master. Second, I was assuming a single step-by-step argument, when in fact Paul was using two short parallel arguments, which come at the subject from different angles but converge at the same conclusion. Between them, you need to mentally insert a phrase like: "Or, instead, think of it *this* way."

Paul is not trying to explain the relationship between the Trinity and us in 6:12–20. Instead, he is incensed that the Corinthians see nothing wrong with doing whatever they want with their bodies, apparently including having sex with prostitutes. In arguing against this, he comes up with objections, rapid-firing them one after the other. What about this? And what about that?

There are other examples of this in 1 Corinthians, but the most complex concerns the resurrection, found in chapter 15. There we find four separate "Oh, and another thing" arguments. Verses 1–12 are the background, in which we see the certainty of Christ's own resurrection, which was common ground between Paul and his readers. Verses 12–23 make the argument that if Christ has been raised then resurrection has a precedent, so you shouldn't object to a future resurrection for yourselves.

Then verses 24–28 present a different argument. It is a convoluted one, but it will have made more of an impact on Paul's readers than on us. It goes like this: if the Old Testament is right in its assertion that all God's enemies will be made his subjects, and if we're right to think that death is an enemy, then it follows that death will be one of the enemies that will be made subject. Hence its defeat, resurrection, is sure.

If that argument is odd, the next one is baffling. "Now if there is no resurrection, what will those do who are baptized for the dead? If the dead are not raised at all, why are people baptized for them?" (1 Corinthians 15:29).

It could hardly be clearer that we are merely eavesdropping on someone else's conversation. Both Paul and the Corinthians must know what "baptizing for the dead" meant in Corinth. It must have had something to do with the believers trying to affect the eternal destiny of people who had died, for Paul's argument is that the practice is inconsistent with not believing in the resurrection. Other than that, we're pretty much in the dark.

Paul does not say that he approves of the practice; he is not arguing for or against it. He is arguing that there will be a future resurrection and that the Corinthians should know that. In padding out his parallel arguments, he includes this one, showing the Corinthians that they are inconsistent in their thinking.

My own guess is that Paul *did not* approve of the Corinthians' practice. But their doubting the future hope is a much bigger and more urgent problem. I think Paul felt that he needed to deal with *that* first, and used any argument he could to do so. Once that was sorted, at a future date, he could sort out the less important matters.

No Christian denomination practices baptism for the dead, though pseudo-Christian cults like the Mormons do. This is the only verse in the whole Bible that mentions it and it documents the practice rather than recommends it.

The final parallel argument in chapter 15 is an argument from Paul's own life and practice; he's betting his life on there being a resurrection – otherwise why risk his neck? Fair point.

You see, though? These arguments just pile up next to each other in a heap. They don't progress one from the other either logically or chronologically. Each has an internal logic, of course; there's nothing wrong with the arguments. It's just how he does things sometimes. Don't let it fool you.

Yes, But . . .

More integral to the letter to the Corinthians, Paul uses a style of arguing that is ideal for dealing with know-it-alls. Disagree with someone who is always sure that they are right and they'll either dig in or shut you off. Your only chance of getting anywhere with them is to agree with them. Or at least *sound* like you're agreeing with them. Or at least *start off* by sounding like you agree with them. And once you've agreed with their statement, you tack on so many qualifications that eventually it comes to mean almost the opposite of what was said in the first place. Now that I've pointed this out to you, you won't be able to read more than a few chapters without laughing. Paul does this over and over.

Take the passage we mentioned before about sexual immorality, 1 Corinthians 6:12–20. It's a classic one. Paul probably even quotes the Corinthians directly: "I have the right to do anything." Perhaps the Corinthians used this very argument to justify their behavior. You or I would have argued with them. "No! Not *anything*. There is right and wrong; there are things you cannot do in good conscience." True, but it would have made the Corinthians titter at your unenlightened, old-fashioned ideas rather than listen to you.

Paul, of course, like us, wants to say No. But because of who he's arguing with, because he understands how they think, he doesn't say "No," he says "Yes, but." "You are absolutely right, guys, you can do anything. You know that. But you probably also know (don't you?) that not all things are profitable."

His next sentence is even more brilliant in its self-deprecatory implication about them. "'I have the right to do anything' – but I will not be mastered by anything." Can you see it? Isn't he great? The Corinthians think of themselves as Spiritual Masters, able to dispatch dismissively the "needs" of their bodies. And where you or I would roar straight in with "You're not the masters, God is the only master. Obey!" Paul instead turns the tables and says, "You're so very right, I believe this too . . . and you're not so weak that you would give in to these temptations and let them master you, are you?" Genius.

It makes for tricky reading sometimes, though, because it involves Paul initially appearing to agree with something he thinks is wrong. Readers who are not careful, who do not recognize this as part of a conversation, can therefore misquote and misappropriate the initial soundbites in the argument.

Take 7:1. Notorious. Paul writes: "It is good for a man not to marry" (my translation; literally "not to touch a woman"!). Does Paul think that? Is that Paul's advice to the Corinthians? Some have certainly thought so through the ages. But not you, I think. Look at what comes before it. Look at what comes after it. My name is spelled G E M M M M P F, remember?

Here's what Paul is really saying. He's got the phone to his ear: "Now for the matters you wrote about . . . uh-huh, yeah, 'It *is* good for a person not to marry' *but* . . . because of this and because of that . . . I say . . . the one who doesn't marry does well and the one who marries does well" (my paraphrase; 7:1–40).

All through the letter it's *Yes, but*. Yes, pagan gods don't really exist or have any power, but we still should distance ourselves from them. Yes, Christianity is full of spiritual wisdom, but we shouldn't be proud or boast. Yes, you are spiritual beings, capable of judging the world, but then why bring each other to the pagan law-courts? Yes, I know you baptize for the dead, but shouldn't that also tell you something about a future resurrection hope? Yes, but . . .

The Corinthians cannot simply dismiss Paul as an argumentative naysayer. He agrees with their "wisdom" and then brings them further. Brilliant. And it is no mere tactic. He does not take this too far, as others might. He does not flatter the Corinthians and allow them to think that they are right in everything, that they are genius spiritual beings, advanced students of a new Zen philosophy. Paul has worked hard at listening and replying, just as we saw with Galatians.

He does not give them what they *want*, he gives them what they *need*. They would love to think of themselves as advanced postgraduate students of their advanced teachers. But Paul tells them that they are more like infants and he is teaching them as a parent would. He doesn't go about his task by deciding what they want and giving them that. Instead he gives them what they need, whether it's what they want to hear or not. But he *is* careful to do so in ways that they can hear and to which they can respond.

He has worked hard at understanding and at finding ways to affirm them before correcting them. Listen to him in 11:2, "I praise you for remembering me in everything and for holding to the traditions just as I passed them on to you." But this is not mere flattery. It is an illustration of what he wants them to be more like than they are already – so that his criticisms will be not "you're falling short of my standards" but "you're falling short of the standards you have shown you can achieve." And, in verse 17, he writes, "In the following directives I have no praise for you, for your meetings do more harm than good." He does both – praise and criticize.

He's willing to be fiercely critical in sarcasm, as we saw in 4:8: "Already you've become kings and queens" (my translation). He doesn't flatter them by allowing them to continue to think that they are advanced students, instead calling them "mere infants in Christ. I gave you milk, not solid food, for you were not yet ready for it. Indeed, you are still not ready" (1 Corinthians 3:1–2).

But, from the very outset, he is also appreciative of their gifts, even gifts that they have taken too far. Remember the thanks/praise section that we saw comes at the beginning of almost all letters, but not in Galatians? Now that you know more about the larger letter of 1 Corinthians, and the issues that Paul is going to being critical of, read the thanks in 1:4–9. See the list of issues? Isn't that amazing? It's almost a table of contents of the rest of the letter.

Yes, but.

Try this next time you need to argue with a know-it-all. Bonus points if you can sneak the word "Corinthians" into the conversation without them knowing why.

The World Doesn't Revolve Around You

There are at least two more ways that Paul combats the Corinthian "I'm special" mentality – two themes that he weaves skillfully throughout the letter, returning to them in different forms, sometimes subtly. They are 1) a stress on traditions rather than innovations and 2) the deliberate choice of love rather than "my rights."

Throughout the letter, Paul combats the Corinthians' feeling that they are exceptional by emphasizing consistency, tradition, and order. His intention is nowhere clearer than the confrontational questions in 4:7 and the echoes found later in 14:36: "Who makes you different from anyone else? What do you have that you did not receive [from someone else]? And if you did receive it, why do you boast as though you did not?" and "Did the word of God originate with you? Or are you the only people it has reached?" Can you hear Paul's attitude in all these questions? "Who the heck do you Corinthians think you are?"

The tradition theme is present from the second verse in the epistle: "To the church of God in Corinth, to those sanctified . . . and called . . . together with all those everywhere who call on the name of our

Lord" (1:2). The Corinthian church is not exceptional, it is one among many.

So also, when Paul talks about Timothy's refresher course, he writes "which agrees with what I teach everywhere in every church" (4:17). When writing about singleness and marriage, he writes, "This is the rule I lay down in all the churches" (7:17). And even on the controversial matter of showing respect in worship by means of head coverings, he writes "we have no other practice – nor do the churches of God" (11:16). He is also careful in that chapter to distinguish his opinions from what is from God (1 Corinthians 7:12; see similarly 7:6, 7:8, and, by contrast, 7:10).

He uses the theme in a similar way to knock down their "I follow Paul" and "I follow Apollos" tendencies, by applying the same thinking to himself. He is, in effect, saying in several places in the letter, "Not only are you Corinthians not exceptional, not innovators, but neither are we apostles. I, Paul, am not exceptional."

This leveling happens most obviously in chapter 3: "What, after all, is Apollos? And what is Paul? Only servants, through whom you came to believe . . . I planted the seed, Apollos watered it . . . The one who plants and the one who waters have one purpose . . . For we are co-workers in God's service" (3: 5–9). Similarly in 15:11, "Whether, then, it is I or they, this is what we preach, and this is what you believed."

This too is the emphasis you'll hear repeated in teaching passages. Remember 11:2? "I praise you for remembering me in everything and for holding to the traditions just as I passed them on to you." He seems deliberately to de-emphasize his own role. He was just passing things along the line. See also the words that precede a sort of creed in chapter 15: "For what I received I passed on to you as of first importance" (15:3). And in the passage concerning the Lord's Supper, there it is again: "For I received from the Lord what I also passed on to you" (11:23).

What do you have that wasn't given to you? And if you were given it, why do you boast?

The business of individuals' rights gets Paul into a lot of trouble with people today. Guaranteeing people their rights is how our culture tries to ensure equality and social justice. But Paul doesn't see things that way. A striking example comes in chapter 7, when, in relation to marriage, Paul makes a statement that was outrageous for his time: "The wife does not have authority over her own body but yields it to her husband. In the same way, the husband does not have authority over his own body but yields to his wife" (7:4). It's outrageous because, contrary to everything in his background, he is making the husband and wife equal in this respect at least. A modern person has trouble with these terms, however. We moderns want equal *rights*; Paul expresses equality as equal *surrender*.

Like us, the Corinthians too think in terms of demanding their rights, as we've seen. Paul teaches them a better way: the way of love and service. It's no mistake that 1 Corinthians 13 is a stand-out chapter. But you'll look in vain there for anything about love demanding its rights. "[Love] is not self-seeking, it is not easily angered, it keeps no record of wrongs" (13:5).

And Paul offers himself as an example of Christian living by giving up rights. In chapter 9, we read about Peter (Cephas) who travels with his wife and apparently expects that the Christians he visits will house and feed them (9:4–6). Behind this reference may be a complaint from the Corinthians themselves, perhaps even their attempt to side with Paul against Peter. It may have gone something like this: "Peter and his wife demand food, but we think you do the Christian thing, Paul, in working for a living. We told the Peter Party that they are wrong."

If so, Paul's reply will have surprised them. For rather than going against the rival teacher (Peter), Paul affirms Peter's right (9:12) but then goes on to say in verses 12 and 15 that although he has the same rights he chooses not to use them. Paul models not an existence without rights, but one in which people give up their rights wherever they think it will help. In the argument about meat offered to idols, he volunteers, "if what I eat causes my brother or sister to fall into sin, I will never eat meat again" (8:13).

Give glory to God, give love and respect to the brothers and sisters, go out of your way to seek the good of the other person, not your own rights. That's the message of 10:31–33, but you see it throughout the letter. Paul is almost baffled that the Corinthians don't see this truth when he writes: "The very fact that you have lawsuits among you means you have been completely defeated already. Why not rather be wronged? Why not rather be cheated?" (6:7).

Throughout 1 Corinthians Paul employs arguments designed to affect the Corinthians. And this is perhaps most telling of all: When he writes to a community where some follow Paul, some follow Peter, and some follow Apollos, Paul refuses to take part in the squabble. He will not argue that he's better than Apollos nor that Peter goes too far in expecting to be supported. If you were Apollos, or if you were Peter, isn't that exactly what you'd hope he would write? Paul again writes exactly the right sort of things – and with panache.

As with the Galatians, he has listened well and replied cleverly and convincingly. And, just as in Galatians, his message is crystal clear and consistent. Or is it? Uh-oh.

Questions for Discussion or Reflection

1. A few chapters ago I asked you to read through 1 Corinthians and try to note any quotations from the Corinthians that Paul recites back to them. Have a look at those notes now and see if there are any I didn't bring up in this chapter, and, if so, whether Paul sets them in a "Yes, but" context.

2. Do you think Paul is truly against innovations in worship, or is it just that he is against those innovations that might lead to the Corinthians thinking that they're superior? Can you prove that your view is right from the text?

3. Recap some of the ways that Paul shows he has really deeply listened to the Corinthians' situation.

10

Pauline "Consistency"

What Counts?

In 1 Corinthians 13, the "love chapter," Paul tells the Corinthians that if they have faith, but don't work that faith out in love, then it's worth nothing (1 Corinthians 13:2). This is a reasonable thing for him to say. The undisciplined, self-centered Corinthians talk big and walk tall – and step all over each other in the process. Christianity isn't about "big." It's not your status that matters; it's about living in harmony with God.

"Circumcision is nothing and uncircumcision is nothing. Keeping God's commands is what counts" (7:19).

Now the interesting thing is that Christians all over the world nod their heads and think, "Yes, that's typical Paul."

It isn't.

Think about it. Don't you remember the quote about circumcision and uncircumcision from Galatians: "Neither circumcision nor uncircumcision means anything; what counts is the new creation" (Galatians 6:15)?

Aren't these two verses diametrically opposed to each other? On the one hand, we've seen that Paul's message to the Corinthians was that their status in Christ doesn't exempt them from having to keep God's commandments. *It's not your status, it's the commands of God, stupid!* But, on the other, it's the reverse: we've seen that his message to the Galatians was to stop worrying about keeping commandments – that they're no longer under the Law; they have a secure status in Christ through the promises and example of Abraham. *It's not the commands, it's your status in Christ, stupid!*

Can this be right? Can the Scriptures really contain such contradiction? Look those verses up in your own Bible if you don't believe me. Oh, but by now, you'll know the two books well enough to know I'm right, don't you?

Skeptics complain that Paul and James contradict each other. Paul harping on about *faith not works saves you* while James going on about *faith without works is dead*, as if in response. Some professors in twentieth-century universities made a good living arguing that there were two rival factions in the early church advocating these two contradictory, mutually exclusive, approaches.

Does the Bible contradict itself? Or, never mind *the Bible*. Doesn't *Paul*, all by himself, contradict himself?

Slavery and Freedom; Power and Weakness

And it gets worse.

In 1 Corinthians 4:1–16, Paul writes about how people should regard Christians as slaves of God, with the apostles on display at the end of the procession. This is an image he draws from ancient military triumphant parades, where the captured opponents, now slaves, are led through the streets with their leaders at the end. To the Corinthians, Paul writes that Christians are servants and slaves.

To the Galatians, though, Paul writes: "It is for freedom that Christ has set us free. Stand firm, then, and do not let yourselves be burdened again by a yoke of slavery" (Galatians 5:1).

Are we slaves or not, Paul?

Or again, when Paul expresses his anger at the Corinthians, in 1 Corinthians 4:8, he sarcastically ridicules them with "Already . . . you have begun to reign . . . !" Instead, by example, he says that their models, the apostles, are like the slaves (4:9), the "scum of the earth" (4:13).

How different to his argument in Galatians that Christians should not think of themselves as slaves any longer. The people of God, as children, may have been little different from slaves. But now the fullness of time has come, we are no longer to be like slaves but like sons and daughters, heirs to the King.

Are we still scum or are we heirs to the throne, Paul?

As we saw, in sarcastic mode, Paul criticizes the way the Corinthians think Christianity is something that they can innovate and improvise: "For who makes you different from anyone else? What do you have that you did not receive?" (4:7) and "I have no praise for you, for your meetings do more harm than good" (11:17). Instead he wants them to treasure and follow traditions (7:17; 11:2,23; 15:3).

But, back in Galatians, he was scalding in his opposition to their desire to once again become slaves to tradition: "It is for freedom that Christ has set us free. Stand firm, then, and do not let yourselves be burdened again by a yoke of slavery" (5:1).

Do we follow traditions or not, Paul?

In the first two chapters of their letter, the Corinthians are told that Christianity is not a matter of being wise or speaking powerfully. Paul would rather they would become foolish and weak (1:27–8; 3:18–19).

But do you remember his letter to the Galatians? "You foolish Galatians!" was a phrase he chucked at them in anger (3:1). They are not to be foolish and weak, but to continue in power.

Are we to be foolish and weak or to display wisdom and power?

Do you remember that in Galatians, Paul was scathing in his treatment of the apostle Peter? Those who were held in high esteem meant nothing to him (2:6). Peter at his best was Paul's equal, offering the right hand of fellowship (2:9), the apostle to the Jews the way that Paul was an apostle to the Gentiles. But at worst, he was someone in the wrong who had to be taken in hand and scolded – publicly (2:11,14).

But, in 1 Corinthians, Peter is presented at worst as an equal, someone with the same rights as Paul (although Paul doesn't exercise those rights, 9:5). But later in the letter, well, Paul admits that he himself is "the least of the apostles" (15:9), which does not sound like equality. The risen Lord Jesus "appeared to James, then to all the apostles, and last of all he appeared to me also, as to one abnormally born" (15:7–8). And to whom did Jesus appear first? Paul doesn't need to say, doesn't need to name names, but he does. In 1 Corinthians 15:5, Paul writes that the resurrected Jesus "appeared to Cephas [Peter], and then to the Twelve."

So which is it, Paul? Is Peter someone deserving of high esteem, chief of the apostles, or is he at best an equal who has a tendency to mess up?

It's clear that Paul wrote two contradictory letters. Or perhaps there were actually two different Pauls? One wrote to the Galatians. He was freedom-loving, anti-tradition, and fiercely anti-law. His mysterious twin wrote to the Corinthians. This Paul longed to impose consistency across the churches and was anti-innovation, pro-tradition, and concerned with ethics and behavior rather than faith in the abstract. To such a one, the Law was not such a bad idea.

Two Pauls, two contradictory and mutually exclusive messages. Could that be right?

Contradiction and Continuity in the Art Museum

But there's another possibility. Once you take notice of the other people in the equation – the Corinthians and the Galatians – then the answer to this riddle comes into focus. As we've said before, don't view Paul's letters as abstract writings setting out a position, see them as letters to real people in real situations, setting out correctives.

So, to take that last example. Paul does not set out in either letter to answer the question, "How do I see Peter?" Instead, in both cases,

Paul mentions Peter only because of how his readers are tending to see Peter or the relationship between Peter and himself. The Galatians, I believe, expect Paul to turn to jelly when he hears that students of Peter disagree with him. When replying to them, Paul needs to say, "Hang on, I am also an apostle, and Peter himself can be wrong." On the other hand, the Corinthians with their cliques might be writing to Paul saying, "You're right, aren't you, Paul? We told those Peter folks, we don't listen to him, we follow Paul!" To combat that attitude, Paul wants to show that Peter deserves respect and that he himself is not against Peter's ministry. If we want to know Paul's real overall attitude to Peter, we get there not by reading either letter, but by reading both, sensitive to the situation behind each letter.

So with many issues. If you take just one letter, and forget to see it in its conversational context, you can think that Paul is dead-set against something. But someone else, using a different letter, outside of its context, thinks that Paul is all for it.

Consider this parable. A top guy at an art museum strolls into one of the galleries with a cloud of his underling curators. He notices that one of the paintings is hanging askew. "Nudge the Renoir to the right!" he orders. They do so; he nods his approval and returns to his office. They are pleased with themselves. "Nudge the Renoir to the right" they all repeat to each other, nodding. And, going around the whole museum, they systematically hunt down every last Renoir in the collection and nudge them to the right. Thus paintings that had been hanging straight for decades are now crooked. One was already tilted unnaturally to the right and their ministrations only made it worse. But they were following their boss's orders. Will he be pleased with them?

The problem is that the underlings are thinking exclusively about their orders in terms of themselves rather than the paintings. Their mantra is "How shall we then nudge? Thusly: to the right." As long as they do so, they'll make this mistake. You can imagine the boss looking at another painting and saying, "Nudge that one to the left." The assistants would hold their head and howl. Contradiction! If the museum chief's advice were primarily about himself and how best to nudge paintings, then his advice is contradictory. But it's not really about nudge and nudgee. It's about paintings and hanging straight. You've got to look at what the boss was looking at to understand the boss's orders. You hear the orders, see the paintings, and conclude, "The boss wants the painting straight." It's about more than the underlings and nudging.

As long as we think exclusively about the content of the Bible in relation to ourselves rather than our contexts, we'll make a similar mistake. But neither Paul nor the boss were thinking about themselves and issuing orders in the abstract. They were thinking about, and responding to, situations. The epistles are conversations, not systematic theology, remember?

Now be careful. When you first come to see this, it's easy to slip into the erroneous position that all ethics are *merely* situational. If Paul is not dishing out one-size-fits-all universal advice then, some argue, all truth must be relevant and determined by the situations. This is a huge error. Some professors made a good living teaching that kind of gospel too.

But a few moments' reflection shows that this conclusion doesn't necessarily follow from Paul's letter writing. The museum boss wants to jog one painting to the left and another a little to the right and still another a lot to the right. Does that mean that he has no abstract ideal of a straight-hanging painting? Of course not. Nor does it mean he's confused and contradicting himself.

Paul has a picture of Peter in his head that is perfectly consistent. Peter is worthy of respect, his approval is worth securing, God has chosen him for a great work among the Jews. But he is also a human being and can make mistakes and be corrected like any other human being. Paul *could have* answered the question "What do you think of Peter?" but we do not have his writing on that question. All we have is his writing on positions that might be caricatured as "Peter and his people know best, don't they?" on the one hand and "Down with Peter; we follow Paul!" on the other.

If the epistles were primarily about Paul himself and his theology, then we've got contradictions. But if the epistles are primarily about the dialogue between Paul and various communities, then the puzzle pieces fall into place. Factor in the communities and the way that they sit on the museum wall. The Corinthians and the Galatians erred in diametrically opposite directions – the Galatians worried that they needed obedience to get them right with God; the Corinthians boasted they were so right with God they could act any way they liked. One was leaning to the left, the other was leaning to the right. Can you imagine Paul doing anything other than saying "Nudge the Galatians to the right; nudge the Corinthians to the left"?

The walls of our museums

Now here's the problem for us. If we want to know how to straighten the painting that is our own community, one group will find an order in Scripture to nudge it to the left, and another will find another order in Scripture to nudge it to the right. And an almighty shoving match ensues. "Look at the text", each side will explode, "it clearly says what to do!"

But that's treating the Bible as a system, as a manual. Remember what we talked about at the very beginning? If God had meant to give us a system, he could have. If he'd meant to give us an advice manual he could have. Instead we've got "other people's mail." And we have to take that seriously. Our problem is that too often we look through the epistles for the bits that resonate with us, the advice that "feels right" and then use it to clobber people who disagree with us.

What should we do instead? We should think "what did it mean?" before "what does it mean?" Here it is in a nutshell: in a controversy, don't search Scripture looking for the advice with which you resonate. Search the Scriptures for the situation that resembles yours and see what advice is given to people in your situation. Is your church fighting over whether the worship service should be traditional or free-form? The traditionalists will use 1 Corinthians with its stress on following traditions like the liturgy of the Lord's Supper and on order and control. The free-formers will pull out Galatians with its sarcasm about being slaves to certain times and seasons and insistence on freedom.

But you need to start by thinking about the congregations: compare yours with the Galatians and the Corinthians. Are you in a situation where people think what saves them are the formalities? Or are you in a situation where people believe that, because they're already free in Christ, self-expression and creativity are what worship is all about? If the former, then give more attention to Galatians and its message of the importance of freedom. If the latter, then pay more attention to Corinthians and the importance of self-discipline and tradition.

Now maybe it's idealistic to think that this would do away with all disagreements about the nature of the congregation. But this method should make it easier and less threatening to see how the Bible and other people might evaluate our own position. To take a personal example: do I overemphasize my Lutheran sacramental view of the Lord's Supper as if it were some all-important test of biblical Christianity, as the teachers of the Galatians treated their view of circumcision? Wouldn't it be better for me to try to work with those I worship with, to show that the Lord's Supper is something important and central and not just an ordinary meal or an afterthought that doesn't matter?

And this method also should make it easier to phrase our objections to other positions in terms of what we want to affirm rather than in terms of what we don't like.

We still need to ask "what it meant" and "what it means" of 1 Corinthians. And we should also ask the same questions about the apparent contradictions that we found. We'll hit those in the next chapter.

Questions for Discussion or Reflection

1. Have you ever been faced with someone who argued that James and Paul contradicted each other (about faith and works)? How did you answer in the past? How would you answer now?

2. Imagine that you're a person living in Corinth and you don't like the way the rest of the church is carrying on. Do you think you'd look forward to the church getting a letter from Paul or not? Suppose all you knew about Paul was his letter to the Galatians; would you expect him to be on your side or not?

3. The two letters, 1 Corinthians and Galatians, are very different and speak to very different situations. But what kinds of things do you read in each that remain constant across the different situations?

11

What Did/Does It Mean?

What It Meant

"Do the Law and gain/keep God's love," said the Galatians. "No," said Paul. "Love God and then do as you please. Your love for God and submission to his Holy Spirit will keep you on the Way."

"Do anything you want now that you have God's love," said the Corinthians. "No," said Paul. "Love God and do as you *then* please. If your focus is on pleasing God rather than yourselves, if you get yourselves to the place where your desire is to build up the church rather than yourselves, you're on the Way."

"Faith expressing itself through love" (Galatians 5:6). That's the key. Is it all just expression? No. Is it all about faith without expressing love? No. To both the Galatians and the Corinthians, it's faith expressing itself through love. See it again in 1 Corinthians 10:31–33: "So whether you eat or drink or whatever you do, do it all for the glory of God. Do not cause anyone to stumble, whether Jews, Greeks or the church of God – even as I try to please everyone in every way. For I am not seeking my own good but the good of many, so that they may be saved."

Each Corinthian needed to stop acting as though they were the only important one; the Corinthian church needed to stop acting as if it was the only important one. Paul wanted Corinthians who gave glory and love to God and respect and love to their fellow believers at Corinth and elsewhere. He was imploring them to bring their behavior into line with those priorities, with that love and respect.

What It Means

What about us? What *does* it mean? The lessons we must learn from 1 Corinthians depend to some extent on how crookedly our paintings hang. Not that you should soften the letter's message according to your particular leanings; rather the opposite. There are many facets of 1 Corinthians and the ones that are meant for you and I are likely to be the ones that we find the least congenial.

If you're anything like me, though, the first lesson we should learn from this letter is that faith without works is dead. Those are James's words rather than Paul's, but it's a reasonable summary of parts of 1 Corinthians; it could fit right into chapter 13: faith enough to move mountains is to no avail without it being worked out. In James 2 the discussion of faith requiring works is preceded by a criticism of how a congregation at a worship service treats each other and visitors in its midst. You cannot get much closer to that late middle section of 1 Corinthians, where the need to work your faith out in love is connected to how the Corinthians' worship services do more harm than good because of the way they treat each other and the implications for the visitors in their midst.

The Lutheranism I grew up with consistently emphasized Galatians – Faith Alone. And Luther himself found James suspicious and didn't really like "that right strawy epistle" being in the canon. But, living as I do in the church of the twenty-first rather than the sixteenth century, I'm in little danger of seeing Christianity purely as a matter of works. My situation, unlike Luther's, resembles Corinth more than Galatia. I don't need to be reminded to "believe," I need to be reminded to act. I don't need the reminder to love the Lord, I need the reminder to do what he says, which he told us was the mark – no, the very definition – of loving him (John 14:15). This letter should challenge me to live out my faith and professed commitment.

We've all heard stories – perhaps we've even featured in the stories – of Christians tsk-tsking while stepping over sleeping homeless people wrapped in cardboard on the steps of the church in order to attend a service in which they hear of Jesus' welcoming acceptance of the outcasts of his day. If I have faith enough to move mountains, but don't work it out through love, then I'm nothing but one of those annoying watch-battery musical chips repeating the same two bars of a hymn in an overpriced greeting card.

The second lesson is related. I think 1 Corinthians is telling us post-modern westerners that we need to love each other and think more in terms of "out-dated" notions of courtesy and respect than in terms of rights and freedoms. Perhaps, for different reasons, we find ourselves in a culture that behaves very similarly to the Corinthians. We want attention; we want the advantages that we believe are our rights. And if anything keeps us from these, we, like the Corinthians, look for sympathy and redress, sometimes even redress in the courts. We might usually return the money when we're given too much change but we always object when we're over-charged, even if it's for something that we think is worth more than we're charged. We want what's ours, not more (although we won't complain) but never, ever less! Despite the example of the parable of the unforgiving servant, sometimes even the most loudly Christian companies will pursue in the courts people too poor to pay up what they owe. We only want what's fair, but we pursue fairness with more tenacity than we pursue generosity.

Many years ago when I worked in a restaurant, none of the waiters wanted the non-smoking section; it was common knowledge that the folks who didn't smoke or drink were the worst tippers. Shouldn't Christians be known as the most generous, the best tippers – not because they have the most money, of course, but because they are the least concerned with clinging to what they do have – and more importantly, the most concerned with honoring others? We tend to have fair-minded but self-centered hearts rather than servant hearts. With attention as well as with currency, we're stingy; our peer group is our audience, but we're willing to share the stage. "You have your turn and I'll listen to you, but then you'd better take your turn and listen to me, or I'll be angry with you."

We've got lots to learn about the self-denial and servanthood that Jesus and Paul described and lived. When Paul tells the Corinthians to imitate him, it is precisely this self-denial that he wants them to learn. "I am not seeking my own good but the good of many so that they may be saved. Follow my example, as I follow the example of Christ" (10:33 – 11:1). Here's an amazing contrast. In Galatians, Paul shows himself equal to and independent of the other apostles: "As for those who were held in high esteem – whatever they were makes no difference to me" (2:6–7, see also 1:1,12,16–17). But Galatia was a community he didn't need to teach about self-denial.

As we've seen, to teach the Corinthians about selflessness, instead of talking about his equality or superiority to Peter, Paul defends Peter where his practice is different to his own (1 Corinthians 9). And, the even bigger surprise, Paul places Peter in the superior position in regard to apostleship, recounting the resurrection appearances as starting with Peter (15:5–8).

Are you like me? I'm not in need of the confidence to disagree with the pillars of my church (as you've doubtless observed from the text of this book so far), I'm in need of the humility to support them even where they differ from me – even at my own expense. Paul does that. Yes, even Paul.

Learning from the Contrast

Remember me asking why it is that the Lord decided to give us so much of the New Testament in the form of various letters to various communities? Here's one of the reasons. As well as the lessons we learn from asking "what does it mean?" from Corinthians and from Galatians, we must also learn from the *contrast* between Corinthians and Galatians.

And, from that contrast, we learn at least two things. First, different people need different corrections. And we have a gospel that can flex. That's not to say it has no shape. Classical twentieth-century liberalism mistook the gospel's flexibility for a Corinthian "anything goes" beanbag chair. They were wrong. Some fundamentalists make the opposite mistake, though, and confuse strength with rigidity. Any materials scientist can tell you that it is brittleness that is more likely to be correlated with rigidity than strength.

You know those building tools with the tube of liquid and a bubble inside called spirit levels? True New Testament faith is more like one of those than a mere straight-edge ruler. It doesn't just stand for straightness against a crooked world. It becomes part of the tilts and slopes in order to testify (unfalteringly and uncompromisingly) to how to straighten out. It's no coincidence if that sounds like the Incarnation.

Second, we begin to learn that every situation can be met with the "law of Christ" or the "law of love" that we call the gospel. That wasn't quite true of the Hebrew Law, at least not the unfulfilled Law that the Pharisees practiced.

Our Method

So the methodology we used for Galatians has also worked well with 1 Corinthians. There is much similarity in terms of form and function at least. We have used the same steps: looking at situation and clues, then looking at Paul's arguments, and then asking what it meant/ what it means. We've discovered a very different situation in Corinth than in Galatia, and for this, not surprisingly, Paul had some radically different advice. Without pausing to consider and understand the situations to which Paul was writing, one might well have concluded that the Bible was contradictory on some of these points.

The reality of the situation, however, is not contradiction but continuity. Holding his end of the conversations with two different churches coming from such different situations, of course Paul's side sounded different. But you'll know all this from your own experience when you share the gospel. You don't just parrot the whole of evangelical theology each time. Your presentation is tailored to meet the needs of the hearer. Talking to a skeptical chemical engineer, you have very different things to say than when speaking to a spiritualist. With the one, you need to struggle to allow that there might be realities beyond what we can measure and test; with the other you have trouble keeping your late Aunt Millicent out of the conversation.

Paul is a genius. He used to be a Pharisee, as rigid as anything. Now he's learnt this flexibility and self-denial from Jesus and with that flexibility comes a new strength. He's able to write letters that express these things. And, more than that, he's able to embody them in himself. Learning this about him from his letters made me like him so much more than I ever did before.

He's not off in some ivory tower preaching about love; he's often writing from prison, living out that love through his letters. He is far from a self-important authoritarian. Even to a community where some groups are claiming him as their guru he places himself far behind his rivals, as one untimely born. That's so good.

Now we've tackled two of Paul's biggest and most important letters. So I think you're ready for an even bigger challenge: the miniscule but outrageous one-page memo to Philemon.

Questions for Discussion or Reflection

1. Is "love God and do as you *then* please" a good motto for the Christian life? What sorts of things are missing from it that you think are crucial?

2. In this chapter I wrote that Christians should be known as the best tippers. In what other "little ways" could Christians exceed expectations?

3. I also wrote that Christians should be like a spirit level, in the slant of the situation but testifying to what is level. Thinking over your life experience, can you think of a Christian who was willing to do this in a way that made a real difference to you or someone else?

PART IV:

Do What's Best – Philemon

12

Runaway!

The third and last of the three letters we'll look at is the letter of Paul to Philemon. It was my teacher, Paul Sampley, who taught me that a pretty amazing thing happens if you let a group of people read it for themselves and draw their own conclusions. Let me tell you about it.

The Runaway and His Owner

The situation takes some getting used to for us today, but it will not have been that unusual in the ancient world – except that the people to whom it happened were Christians. *That* would have been unusual.

This tiny letter was indeed written to a friend of Paul's named Philemon. He was a wealthy enough man to own slaves, one of whom was named Onesimus, whose name, translated, is something like "useful" or "handy."

Except Onesimus wasn't all that useful. In fact, he was a runaway and a thief. In fact, simply by being a runaway, he became a thief. If a slave is your property, you see, when they run off, they are making away with your property. Thus, Onesimus stole himself.

You can see why slaves might want to steal themselves. And Onesimus, like many runaway slaves before and after, went to the big city to try to lose himself and perhaps find a new identity. Poor "Handy" though; he did not prove himself to be all that useful at being a runaway, for when he hit the big city, somehow, he ran straight into Paul, a close friend of his master. And probably while in Paul's company, Onesimus converted and became a Christian.

Paul, as someone who had found stolen property, was of course legally obliged to send that property back to its rightful owner. And the custom in those days would have been to punish any returned runaway slave severely, probably beating him to within an inch of his life and then giving him all the nastiest jobs from then on. He'd spend the rest of his life making himself "handy" cleaning the toilets with the family's old non-electric toothbrushes.

That's what would normally happen. But both the slave and the slave owner are now Christians; is that how Christians should act toward each other?

Paul does send Onesimus back. But ahead of Onesimus' arrival, he sends the letter we now have in our Bibles as "Philemon." It is a letter alerting the slave owner to the imminent return of the runaway. But what does Paul want his old friend to do? What behavior is the letter to Philemon suggesting?

I wonder if you'd be willing to do what I ask my students to do; close this book now, and read the letter as if you yourself were Philemon. What would you do?

Structure and Center

Remember that, when we looked at 1 Corinthians, we saw that Paul does not always employ outlined, logically structured forms. We saw him using what I called "parallel arguments." In fact, Paul, like most ancient writers or speakers, had a variety of structures to choose from, like templates. These would not be mapped out painstakingly as if it were a choreographed performance, but, rather, as a person spoke or wrote, the material would tumble out in one of the forms or another. They are more like habits or conventional ways of telling something rather than carefully followed blueprints.

In the twenty-first century, we tend to work this way with outlines or bullet points. Even when we don't deliberately try to do so, our talks and even informal letters follow the pattern of main points with subsidiary points underneath them. Some of you might even find this pattern so deeply ingrained that you wonder if I'm making too much of this – as if there are any other ways of constructing anything.

But there are. And I believe Paul more or less falls into one of the others in this letter: a pattern called "chiasm" because it follows the contour of the left side of the Greek letter chi, which looks like a stretched-out X. The point of a chiasm is its symmetry. It starts outside then delves step-by-step all the way in to the center of the topic but then traces the implications all the way out again, again step-by-step, with steps that echo the way in.

Occasionally I catch contemporary authors and songwriters using chiasms, in passages like: "The little hairs on the back of my neck all stood up when I looked into the barber shop mirror. I saw myself in the chair across the shop, looking in the barber shop mirror, with the little hairs on the back of my neck all stood up."

Can you see the structure?

A The little hairs on the back of my neck all stood up
   B when I looked into the barber shop mirror.
      C I saw myself in the chair across the shop,
   B´ looking in the barber shop mirror,
A´ with the little hairs on the back of my neck all stood up.

I doubt that these writers had any Greek letters or ancient literary patterns in mind when they penned passages like this. In this particular case, the author could have been thinking that the form suited the content of mirrors within mirrors, but it does illustrate a chiastic form nicely, tunneling into the subject, then back out again.

When Paul or other ancient authors used this form, they used it as unconsciously as we use outline/bullet points. It may be that the form is not perfectly carried out because the author/speaker is not using it consciously or as a stencil to guide their pen strokes, but rather that it is so deeply ingrained that when they're talking, the material falls naturally into that form, like you, if asked to write a song, would find yourself employing a *verse chorus verse chorus verse* sort of pattern without really thinking, "I must be sure to include a repeating refrain."

Here, I think, is how Philemon falls into this pattern:

A Formal epistle stuff (vv.1–3)

  B Prayer of Paul for Philemon (vv.4–6)

    C Philemon's hospitality (v.7)

      D Authority (v.8)

        E Supplication (vv.9–10)

          F Onesimus, a convert of Paul (v.10)

            G Wrong done by Onesimus, amends by Paul (vv.11–12)

              H To receive Onesimus = to receive Paul (v.12)

                I Paul, Philemon (vv.13–14)

                  J Onesimus' new standing (v.15)

                  J′ Onesimus' new standing (v.16)

                I′ Paul, Philemon (v.16)

              H′ To receive Onesimus = to receive Paul (v.17)

            G′ Wrong done by Onesimus, amends by Paul (vv.18–19)

          F′ Philemon, a convert of Paul (v.19)

        E′ Supplication (v.20)

      D′ Authority (v.21)

    C′ Philemon's hospitality (v.22)

  B′ Prayer of Philemon for Paul (v.22)

A′ Formal epistle stuff (vv.23–25)

Although it's not exact, can you see how point A echoes A′ as does each following point all the way in to the center? And that center is, of course, the thing Paul wants most to say, which is, in effect: your relationship with Onesimus has changed (vv. 15–16). Each step leads all the way in to that and there are implications that are traced all the way out again.

Hopefully you will have read the letter by now and be familiar enough with it to have a pretty clear idea of what Paul wants you, Philemon, to do and how he's convincing you to do that, yes? If not, this might be a good time to spend time thinking about that before going on to the next section.

Strong Language

Whenever I ask a group to read the letter and decide what Paul wants them to do, they always come back to me wanting to talk about something else even more. If you've read the book as Philemon yourself, you're probably feeling the same way. You'll think: Paul is laying it on a bit thick.

And you're right. There is incredibly strong language here. In a large group of students I can count on two particular phrases being volunteered from the crowd.

The first is "manipulation."

Look at the compliments heaped up in verses 5 and 7: Paul hears of the love you, Philemon, have for all God's people, a love that has brought such joy and encouragement and refreshing. But anyone who has any experience with authority can't help noticing what comes next.

These positive statements flow directly into verse 8: "Therefore . . ." Uh-oh. Paul reminds you that it wouldn't be improper for him to *order* you to do something. But he "prefers" to *appeal* to you on the basis of love.

And see what he does next? "I appeal to you on the basis of love . . . Me . . . Paul . . . an old, frail man, someone who is willingly suffering hardships in prison for Christ Jesus while you are warm and safe at home . . . I, Paul, am asking you to do something." Yikes! "Don't worry about me . . . I'll be okay" (my paraphrase).

The second phrase that tends to come up is "emotional blackmail," and I think you can see where such a feeling comes from. Look at verses 18–19 for an example: "If this runaway slave has done you any harm, if he owes you anything charge it to me, Paul, and I promise you that I will pay it back" (my paraphrase).

Next comes a phrase that no one ever likes to hear. "Not to mention . . ." Why does anyone say that? You can't say it unless you in fact fully intend to mention what you say you're not. If Onesimus owes you anything, charge it to my account and I swear I will pay you back, not to mention the fact that when we look at "our accounts," you already are massively in my debt, Philemon, old pal. You owe me your very soul.

Then he adds in verse 21, "Confident of your obedience, I write to you, knowing that you will do even more than I ask."

Community Pressure

Plus, get this: have you noticed that this letter is clearly not meant to be read by Philemon alone, in the privacy of his smoking room? Look at verses 1 and 2 . . . the letter is meant to be read by Philemon, of course, but also by Apphia (who some people think is Philemon's wife. If you want someone to do something, ask them in front of their spouse) and Archippus . . . and – okay, why not? – read it in front of the whole church! Can you imagine yourself in Philemon's sandals at a public reading of this letter? Philemon, you are so wonderful, full of love . . . so I know that you'll do this little thing for me, not to mention that everyone here now knows that you owe me, big time.

How embarrassing.

And that's not the end of it, either. Verse 22 makes things even worse. The slave is on his way to you. You're going to have to make a decision and do something within the next week, probably. And then . . . Oh, by the way, Paul slips in just before the end, get a guest room ready for me because I myself will be there soon (to see what decision you've made and how you're treating the slave).

Wow! This is a writer at the peak of his powers; he knows exactly what he's doing, doesn't he? This isn't a letter so much as it is a twenty-five-verse avalanche, and Paul has enlisted the whole congregation of the church in the snow job.

You're probably wondering how a chapter like this is meant to induce you to like Paul. Hold on to your hat in the next chapter.

For now, everyone in the congregation is staring at you expectantly. The question is, what is Paul expecting you to do? The answer is, I think, going to surprise you.

Questions for Discussion or Reflection

1. Just for fun, try to list some of the major events of your day yesterday first as an outline and then, a little bit more difficult for most of us, as a chiasm . . . with sleeping at the beginning and end, or maybe commuting to and from somewhere at the beginning and end.

2. Do you agree that Paul is piling on a lot of pressure? Does it seem excessive?

3. Before reading any further in the book, try to guess what you would do if you were Philemon and how the people around you might react.

– 13 –

Make it So

A writer at the peak of his powers, using those considerable powers to force you to do what he thinks is right, yes? But what is that? Let's have a look.

Send Him to Paul

It seems to us an odd idea that a person could "steal" themselves, but we have seen that, since slaves were property, that was a logical consequence. By that same logic, then, it was possible to give people as gifts. And, in fact, this seems to have happened often.

Now Paul, remember, paints himself as a somewhat pathetic figure at the moment . . . in prison. Paul is needy, Philemon, and what are you doing to help him? Why aren't you there? Through your slave, you can be! Paul writes, ". . . he could take your place in helping me while I am in chains for the gospel" (v.13). He presses this again in verse 20: "I do wish . . . I may have some benefit from you."

So, when Paul reminds you, Philemon, in verse 19, "you owe me your very self," isn't he suggesting: "you owe me a life . . . a person"? Is Paul not making the solution obvious? You owe me a person; here is a person you have at your disposal; why not let him take your place in helping me?

There's another facet to this that would occur to you if you were actually Philemon. A returned runaway slave who is a new Christian presents a problem. If, because of all that pressure from Paul, you do begin to treat him as a brother and don't treat him like dirt as expected, your other slaves will, without doubt, sense the "Get Out Of Jail Free" card that this represents.

But . . . if you can quickly and quietly send him to Paul and the rough life that Paul is having, he becomes less of a living reminder to the other slaves that one can run away and, even if the escape fails, still be treated well.

Clearly, this is the solution: send him back to Paul, yes?

Not so fast.

Keep Him and Esteem Him

Paul is playful with the language here. Remember how the Greek word "Onesimus" actually translates to something like "handy"? Look at verses 10 and especially 11: ". . . I appeal to you on behalf of Handy . . . Formerly he was a handful for you, but now he has become as handy to you as he has to me" (my paraphrase). He is going to become useful to you, presumably, because his attitude toward his work will change now that he is a Christian.

Some translations render the last part of verse 11 as "useful both to you and me," which remains ambiguous. I think the wording of the Greek actually suggests a translation more like "now to you as he has to me" and the parallel verse, verse 16, cements that sort of emphasis: "He is very dear to me but even dearer to you."

So, although at first we thought Paul was saying he wanted Onesimus with him, perhaps that was only the first part of the clause – an endorsement: I find him useful, so I'm sure you will as well.

After all, verse 15 is pretty unambiguous, isn't it? "Perhaps the reason he was separated from you for a little while was that you might have him back forever."

But wait . . . there's more . . .

Send Him to Paul

Perhaps ancient culture and decorum prevent Paul from actually asking for what he wants; perhaps we need to read between the lines. He clearly indicates that he is refraining: ". . . I could be bold and order you to do what you ought to do, yet [or but] . . ." (vv.8–9).

We must not read too much into the fact that Paul is sending Onesimus back after the letter, as he would have been obliged by law to do so. "I am sending him . . . back to you. I would have liked to keep him with me" (vv.12–13). Although he would have liked to keep Onesimus, that would have not only been impolite, but illegal.

Paul therefore writes in verse 14, "I did not want to do anything without your consent, so that any favor you do would not seem forced but would be voluntary."

And even though he declines to make demands of obedience, Paul writes near to the end of the letter, "Confident of your obedience, I write to you, knowing that you will do even more than I ask" (v.21). Does he mean "even more than I can politely ask"?

Surely, Philemon, you are supposed to send this slave as a favor and gift to Paul, thus doing more than he can politely and legally ask?

But then again . . .

Keep Him and Esteem Him

Paul is clearest about you welcoming back, rather than giving away: "if you consider me a partner, welcome him as you would welcome me" (v.17). Surely that's not consistent with giving him as a gift.

And you're not only to welcome him back but "back forever . . . both as a fellow man and as a brother in the Lord" (vv.15–16).

There's another fun word theme that you might not have noticed when you first read the letter. When Paul is buttering up Philemon at the beginning, one of the phrases he uses in verse 7 concerns the heart: "You . . . have refreshed the hearts of the Lord's people." This is reflected back toward the end of the epistle, in verse 20: "Refresh my heart in Christ."

Ah, but how should you refresh Paul's heart in Christ? What does he mean by that? Look at verse 12: "I am sending him – who is my very heart – back to you." It is not his own benefit that Paul is seeking with this phrase, it is Onesimus' benefit. If Onesimus is Paul's heart, you refresh Paul's heart by refreshing Onesimus.

Inconclusive?

We've swung back and forth between two opinions of what Paul wants you to do, Philemon. And this is precisely what will happen if you ever have a chance, as I do, to take a large group of people and break them down into small groups to decide this point. When you come back as a large group to discuss the findings of the discussion, you will find that there is unanimity about the pressure that Paul is applying. Even if you didn't ask people to look for that, they'll find it, and all agree.

But then, when you ask the group what this pressure, this "manipulation," this "emotional blackmail," is meant to force you to do . . . well . . . there is not unanimity, rather at least two factions: some groups that believe Onesimus should go back to Paul and others that think he is to stay on as a well-treated slave. Others will argue that he should be freed ("no longer as a slave" [v.16]).

Before even thinking about which answer is right, consider how very strange it is that this disagreement should arise. How is it that a writer so skilled at persuasion as Paul has been in Galatians and 1 Corinthians, and as clear as he's been about pressure-points here in Philemon, fails to make clear what it is that he wants you to do? We said that Paul was a writer at the peak of his powers, using those considerable powers to force you to do what he thinks is right.

But maybe that's not really the case.

Ajar

Maybe Paul is not trying to force you to do what *he* thinks is right after all. It is so normal for us that you probably didn't notice how cynical most of us are when we read. So people today hear a phrase like "confident . . . you will do even more than I ask" (v.21) and assume that this is controlling or manipulative. Similarly, we rarely give words like the "perhaps" in "Perhaps the reason he was away for a while is so that you might have him back for good" (v.15; my paraphrase) its full innocent force, assuming that writers say "perhaps" as a way of introducing things about which they are actually sure but don't expect you to be.

This might break all of your preconceived biases against Paul, but try it on for size and see if you do not find that it fits the evidence best: what if Paul does not know what the best thing to do is? What if Paul is really, honestly, genuinely, leaving the question open or at least ajar? What if Paul is leaving it open for you?

Is that not the best explanation for why such a good writer should leave us in such doubt about what to do?

But, if that is the case, how can we explain the universal and over-whelming feeling that Paul is piling on pressure as we discussed in the previous chapter?

Simple. The pressure is *not* forcing you to comply with Paul's solution. The pressure is to keep you from doing the obvious, unthought-through, wrong thing. You may *not* beat Onesimus within an inch of his life, and treat him as an object lesson. Paul expects better of you. But what that "better" is, you have only possibilities, not a blueprint.

So it is not really blackmail, not really manipulation. There is no one thing that Paul is forcing you to do. This Paul that you may have thought was hierarchical, authoritarian, and who only saw things in black and white . . . this Paul is saying, "Here's a situation. Let your new relationship with God through Christ change everything and . . . surprise me."

Part of what Paul and the Bible are saying is "surprise me"! How cool is that?

And that's the answer to the first of our twin questions; *that* is what it meant. We have been investigating what it meant in its own setting so far, tentatively setting to one side what it means today. Before we think about today briefly, let me ask you something: was it boring? When we studied God's word for its own sake, without going out of our way to think about "relevance" and "application," did you find it dull or lifeless? And is it really something that doesn't touch you or affect you? Don't you learn about God and your fellow Christians this way? Is that likely to be good or bad for you: to think about others without much thought for yourself?

But of course there are messages here for us today too. I'll briefly sketch three. First, *responsibility*. One of the primary messages of Philemon is that Christians have a responsibility to live out their faith – and when it's not crystal clear how to do so, we must also work out the "how" for ourselves.

The second concerns *faith* and *trust* in each other. Paul shows us that Christian community, and even Christian leadership, should include a deep trust and respect for each other. Many Christian leaders find delegating hard; even when some leaders decide what is best, they have trouble leaving it for others to carry out. But Paul goes beyond this, as we should. Paul exhorts and then trusts Philemon to *decide* what is best *and* carry it out.

Third, I think that there might be a message here for some of us about *assertiveness*. Don't you hate it when you're in a big group in town and you ask, "So. Where shall we eat?" and everyone is too shy to answer in any way except: "Oh, anywhere is fine" and "whatever you think." And then you pick a seafood place and half of them don't like seafood, but didn't want to say anything; and one really liked the look of that Italian place three blocks back? We have seen in this chapter that Paul is a good enough communicator that he managed to suggest several outcomes that he'd like but without truly forcing Philemon toward any particular *one* of them. I'd like to be more like that, wouldn't you? That is, able to make our requests known to God and friends without manipulating them to cater to our wishes.

So, are you liking Paul yet? In our final chapter, I'll share my top eight reasons for doing so. But first, some historical and sociological asides: a question that you are probably wanting to ask me: why doesn't the Bible come right out and condemn slavery? And another question that, for some reason, you almost certainly have not thought to ask me.

Questions for Discussion or Reflection

1. When is it appropriate for Christian leaders to take decisions themselves and when should they leave matters open for others to decide?

2. Isn't it strange that a book like Philemon is in the Bible?! Are there other books that surprise you? What do you think it says about God, that he would build a Bible this way?

3. How can we tell when we've gone from assertive to demanding or arrogant?

– 14 –

Slavery

There are many questions that our twenty-first century raises that aren't addressed directly in Scripture. We want to know what the Bible says about these questions with the same intensity that a Philemon might have wanted to know what Paul wanted him to do with situations pressing in his day. We must, of course, seek clear biblical answers to questions that the biblical writers explicitly address. But when we encounter questions about which they are not explicit, we must try, Philemon-like, to discern how to apply Christian principles to our situations.

Rather than giving you *my* opinion on issues that are controversial in our day, the context of our discussion of Philemon leads us to first explore a less controversial issue about which Scripture seems to be vague, but which most westerners agree on. Today all Christians agree that slavery is wrong. But Scripture never condemns it. Why not? Does that mean slavery is okay?

Of course, when we ask why Paul did not condemn slavery, we cannot answer with any certainty. Why does *anyone* not do something they might have done? We can only speculate. But spending a little time thinking about ancient culture might make what he writes and doesn't write more understandable.

The Invisibility of the Normal

The first thing to say is that slavery could be found everywhere in the ancient world. I mean everywhere. We read in Lysias of a man who pleads poverty in court by describing himself as disabled, claiming a state pension and being too poor to buy even a single slave to work for him. A later public speaker named Libanus describes the plight of destitute lecturers, who must rent a place to live, have debts, and have only a couple of slaves. Slavery was not an institution about which one had an opinion. It was just part of life.

Let me give an example from our culture. In his book *Mere Christianity*, C.S. Lewis mentioned in passing that the ancient Greeks, the Old Testament Jews, and the great Christian teachers of the Middle Ages were united in condemning what is sometimes called "usury." What that word means is, quite simply, lending money at interest – investment. Lewis does not make a recommendation that we condemn the whole concept of interest and investment and purge our society of it. Where in the world would you start? How?

Understand, please: I'm not talking about whether this is a good idea or a bad one, just that it is so wide-ranging as to be virtually unthinkable. We cannot really imagine our world without investment and interest; but other cultures were able to imagine such a world easily. We are in the reverse situation with slavery. We think it should be condemned, and with good reason. But it was so much a part of the fabric of first-century life that condemning the whole system simply would not have occurred to most people, and would not have seemed a practical possibility to those to whom it had.

What happens in such cases when a member of such a culture notices the inequity is that they draw a distinction between good and bad examples of the institution. We thus have "ethical" investments and those that profit from, say, arms sales. So also, in the ancient world, a line was drawn between slaves who were reasonably treated and who could be expected to be grateful that they did not have to worry about food or shelter or clothing thanks to the provision of a good master, and those who were driven mercilessly and beaten unreasonably.

Clearly, it is right to tackle abuses within a system, but in some cases this is like attacking the symptom rather than the disease. Like Paul in 1 Corinthians, sometimes Christians need to pick their battles wisely.

Focus on People and Situations

Paul focused on the situations in front of him and the possibilities open to him. In theory, in western-style democracies, any citizen could stand for political election, and, in theory, influence policy and law-making. And, again, in theory, every citizen votes and has a chance, through selective voting, of that degree of influence. In theory, your ideas matter. If the worst came to the worst, there's always the option to march in protest or strike.

None of this was the case in the same way in Imperial Rome. Holding office could be linked directly to your financial status and, in any case, most offices were ceremonial. Unless you had the sympathetic ear of the Emperor, you were not likely to accomplish anything as a citizen or even Senator. Not only was ancient culture very used to the idea of slavery, it was very *unused* to the idea of ordinary people having any say in law-making or policy-making.

It is worth noting that when Christianity finally *does* have the ear of the Emperor, with Constantine in the fourth century, policies and laws *really do* begin to change. In Paul's day, there were laws dating back to the Emperor Augustus that forbade a slave owner to free more than one-fifth of his slave workforce. Under Constantine, that was dropped and slaves were given rights.

Paul did not have that kind of access or influence in his lifetime. You've seen how the Apostle Paul works across three epistles. You know the old saying: "Give me the courage to change the things I can change, the grace to accept those that I can't, and the wisdom to know the difference." That sentence could have been written as a description of what Paul seems to do unconsciously. Paul *can* speak in general principles, but he seems to excel at focusing not on the abstract rules or theology but on particular people and situations and the practical.

Paul worked at changing the kinds of things that he could change. He did not lead protest marches against the institution of slavery. Instead he seems to have focused on individual people and situations, urging not only the avoiding of abuse, but injecting a new perspective into particular slave–master relationships. To say "welcome him as you would welcome me" (v.17) and "no longer as a slave, but better than a slave, as a dear brother" (v.16) is as radical and revolutionary as any protester's handmade banner.

Strategic Undermining

Paul does not stay silent about the institution while condemning clear abuses. He does more than that. As I said, Paul *can* and does speak about the general: "There is neither Jew nor Gentile, neither slave nor free, nor is there male and female, for you are all one in Christ Jesus." (Galatians 3:28, see also Colossians 3:11), but Paul really finds his voice and the sphere *within* situations rather than outside of them. In many ways, he does not abandon the society and attempt to design and implement a new one, but rather seems to change the structures and meanings of the situations he is in.

Thus, Paul does not try to eliminate slavery from without, but rather attacks the injustices in it from within. And his advice can be phrased in a way that makes clear how little difference there is between the logical outcome of the two strategies: If masters keep slaves, they must regard them as human beings, not as mere property, not as something different from free people.

F.F. Bruce wrote about Philemon in particular that Paul has brought about an atmosphere in which the practice of slavery could only wilt and die. If slaves are equal in God's eyes to a free people, then they must be treated the same and there are much fewer advantages to slave labor.

Paul, albeit without access to channels of institutional power, has used the influence he has with slave owners to eat away at the foundation of the institution. He has not just attacked the symptoms, nor has he merely attacked the institution, he has attacked the root error that underlies the institution and the symptoms: the error that some people can regard other people as things and not as people in God's eyes.

On the one hand, it is possible to be critical of Paul and say that if he had been more outspoken and explicit, the practice of slavery would not have carried on in later centuries, at least in Christian-based societies. But the other hand is full of replies. We can all think of things that are clear in the Bible, yet are still ignored or rationalized around. The fact is that without those things that Paul *did* write, the official abolition of slavery might never have happened.

When you face contentious twenty-first century questions, pause and imagine you lived long ago, when slavery was an undecided question. Appropriating clues from Scripture and living out faith was hard then; it's hard now; it will be hard in every decade before the Lord's return. But it is our responsibility (and no small honor) that we are called to do even more than we are explicitly asked.

Oh; One Last Question You Forgot to Ask

I also said there was a question that you probably didn't think of. It's the question that would have interested someone like Paul even more than the big policy question. It is this: these events we hear about in Paul's letters . . . they really did happen. So what really happened next? What did the real Philemon do when Onesimus showed up back in town? Real people and real situations are what interested Paul.

Don't you find it strange that most of us don't think to ask that? Does it show that we unconsciously do not think of the Bible as containing real stories about real people? Or is it just that we don't really care that much about them?

Unfortunately, having asked the question, I have to admit once again: we don't know the answer. Onesimus is also mentioned in Colossians 4:9, but not in a way that gives us much of a clue as to the resolution of the matter, especially since the likelihood is that Colossians was written before Onesimus went back.

We do have a possible clue from decades later, however, and the romantic in me likes to believe that it relates and ties up the loose ends.

The early Christian writer Ignatius wrote to people in this same area in around AD110, not quite fifty years after the events we've looked at. And in his letter, he writes about how fortunate they are to have such a wonderful bishop over them. And the bishop he names is Bishop Onesimus.

Okay, okay . . . it's a good many years after, and Onesimus was already a fairly common name in Paul's time; the episode described in the letters may have made it an even more popular name among Christians. Ignatius never says he used to be a slave. It could easily be a different man with the same name.

But the timing *could* work. It can't be proven from the available evidence, but I like to believe that in this way Paul's optimism and trust were shown to be justified: Philemon had allowed something to happen that went way beyond what Paul could have ordered or asked for. The guy who was once a useless slave became a treasured spiritual leader in the same community.

Questions for Discussion or Reflection

1. Think about how easy it would be to defend slavery from the Bible. If you're in a group setting, you might even try a pretend debate.

2. The slavery issue is settled; almost all Christians think it's wrong. What are some contemporary questions that Paul doesn't try to answer and about which there are still debates? Does the resolution of the slavery issue help us with a method for solving other problems?

3. Why is it that we can care so much about fictional characters in books or TV shows, yet find it so hard to care what happened to an Onesimus from the Bible? What kinds of things in our culture have de-sensitized us to people in the Bible?

PART V:

Conclusion

– 15 –

Why to Like Paul

If you've arrived here after reading the book, you'll know it's quite a journey we've been on together. If you've snuck straight here without reading the rest of the book, well, you won't agree with much of what follows and I wouldn't expect you to. Don't make up your mind from this conclusion alone.

What is Scripture?

The Bible may not be what you used to think it was. Stop thinking it's about you. God didn't write it about you.

Look. God gave commandments, right? Those are sort of about you – about how you should live. Isn't it odd, though, that the Jews didn't just take the tablets of stone as Scripture? Didn't just see the words that God spoke to Moses as Scripture? Instead, Jews and Christians take the *whole story* surrounding the giving of the Law as Scripture.

God could, of course, have taken a Paul or anyone else and sat them down and dictated Scripture through them the way that he dictated the commandments. Jesus could have returned from his baptism and wilderness experience and grabbed a pen and started writing: "My words are not for this people nor this generation alone but for all people in all ages."

Know what? Many Christians actually would have preferred it that way. But God, clearly, thought there was a better way. A Scripture that is for you, without being about you, directly. A story that is not your story, but important because it is someone else's story.

Paul doesn't say the things that you want him to say. At least, when you're thinking about *yourself* and about here and now, he doesn't say the things that you want him to say. It's hard to feel like he's one of the good guys. It's hard to feel he's on your side. But remember what we said at the beginning – you don't pick your friends (I hope) by whether they agree with you on every issue, but by whether you can respect their values, priorities, and motives.

And one of the most important things, perhaps *the* most important thing, that I hope you will have picked up from this book is the importance of asking, "what did it mean?" *before* asking "what does it mean?"

So stop, for a while. Stop only thinking about yourself and your situations. Stop and think about him and the situations he was in. What would you have done? What would you have said? The Galatians were on the brink of forcing all the males in the congregation to go through a painful operation in order to become more spiritual. What would a good guy do in response? The Corinthians saw nothing wrong with using slave-girl prostitutes and suing the daylights out of each other. What would a good guy do? What would you have written to them? Can you respect Paul's values and motives and ability to communicate them?

If you faced the questions and situations Paul faced, you would be so glad to have him on your side. Walk in his sandals and you'll be amazed at how he can kick.

Can You Like Paul?

I think you *can* like Paul. The *real* Paul, I mean. His harshest critics haven't really listened to him. He's not some authoritarian power-monger looking to sell his quasi-Jewish ideas and practices, persuading through bullying argument if he can, threatening and forcing where he can't. I can understand how you might think that if all you'd read were bits of letters without thinking about what's behind them – snippets read out in Sam Jones (not his real name)'s church. But now that you've been inside three whole letters, you know better.

From what we've looked at together, here are eight reasons for liking Paul.

1) Paul is totally committed to Christ: to knowing him and sharing him.

2) Paul does not think he knows God's truth about everything. Some stuff, yes – we've seen him speak his mind pretty straightforwardly in Galatians. But we've also seen him hold off in Philemon. And we haven't specifically mentioned these verses before, but how strange it is that one of the authors of the Bible should write 1 Corinthians 7:25: "[On this matter] I have no command from the Lord, but I give a judgment."

3) Paul was courageous and a doer and a stand-up-and-be-counted-er. He practiced all that he preached and then some. Never in his letters did he tell someone to do anything as dangerous as the things that he himself had done. Never. He spoke up, he spoke out, he went to where the stuff needed doing and he did it.

4) Paul was sacrificial in his leadership. Christianity has become so big in the history of the world since Paul's time that his modern critics can't help but think that becoming an early Christian leader was a stepping up in status and authority if not salary. Well, it wasn't. In becoming a Christian, Paul gave up all the respectability that he would have expected if he'd stayed on the fast track of Jewish leadership. And he gave up all the financial and material comfort that would have come his way in the Jerusalem inner circle. He joined a penniless, renegade sect that seemed to Paul's own mentor, Gamaliel, doomed to go nowhere. And, as far as we know, he never sought and certainly never received any officially acknowledged leadership

position within that sect. You've seen him argue passionately in 1 Corinthians that he *not* be considered as a more important leader than Peter/Cephas or Apollos.

5) This is one of the biggest ones for me and perhaps the biggest surprise when I realized it was the case: Paul is an even better listener than he is a writer. Paul really and truly listened to the communities to which he wrote. To a striking degree, his letters are much more about the community to whom he is writing and their ideas and terms than they are about his own. When I think of my own writing and teaching, I am put to shame. Paul astounds me.

6) When there is a difference, Paul gives what is needed rather than what is wanted. And he has listened carefully enough to know which is which. His "yes, but" style of arguing in 1 Corinthians shows us that he knows how to play the game, but he plays it honestly and caringly. He does not pretend that he (or Christianity) gives them what they've always wanted. He is no salesman. He would rather critique their desires and give them what they need.

7) Paul is a consummately clever and creative writer. He applies his imagination when he constructs examples and uses techniques designed to make sense to his audience and to communicate clearly and effectively. He can be sarcastic, he can be stern, he can be poetic enough to compose the love chapter 1 Corinthians 13, or blunt enough to omit the standard letter-form thanksgiving and launch in with "I am astonished that you are so quickly deserting" (Galatians 1:6).

8) What we can gauge of Paul's treatment of other people is exemplary. I'm thinking here not only of Philemon, but take the most difficult case: Peter. For much of the twentieth century, many influential scholars thought of Paul as antagonistic to Peter. They were seen as enemy leaders of rival church factions. Galatians was frequently used as a proof text in which Paul reveals his true colors. "[Peter] stood condemned" (2:11).

See? Enemies, right? Only if you discount or re-interpret all other evidence and ignore the situations behind the letters. Even Peter is likely to have thought that the Galatians were putting too much stock in Jewish practices. To such a congregation, Paul writes that when Peter started to go too far, he was brought back to account. Mark's Gospel portrays Peter similarly (Mark 8:29–33; 9:5–6).

But look at how different and more tempting for Paul the situation is in Corinth. There, some people follow Paul and some people follow Peter. If Paul really and truly thought of Peter as opposition – that his way and Peter's way diverged and Peter was wrong and he, Paul, was right – how would he have written 1 Corinthians? Would he not have written as he did in Galatians: showing everyone in Corinth that he was right and Peter was wrong? Instead, as we've seen, Paul calls himself the least of the apostles and implies that Peter is the first (1 Corinthians 15:8 compared with 15:5). And instead, Paul takes what may have been a Paul-Party complaint about Peter – that he expects himself and his wife to be supported materially – and defends Peter and his practices (1 Corinthians 9:4–14).

Thus when writing to a congregation in which there are likely to be people criticizing Peter, we find Paul supporting and defending Peter. It is when there are no Peter critics in the audience that Paul criticizes Peter, and – look – he goes out of his way to tell us that he is not saying anything behind Peter's back that he was not willing to say to Peter's face ("When I saw that they were not acting in line with the truth of the gospel, I said to Cephas . . ." [Galatians 2:14]).

He doesn't always think like you think. He'll confront you face-to- face when he disagrees. He doesn't always do things the same way you do. But when he writes to others about you in your absence, readers who are choosing sides between you and him, he *defends* you and *defends* your different practices. And he tells his readers that, if anything, you deserve more esteem than he does. Wow.

Would Paul Like You?

But all this time I've been sitting in judgment on Paul – is he someone I am willing to like? Maybe you've been thinking like that too – as if you or I were the center of the universe and our willingness to like him matters. What happens if we turn the question on its head: would Paul like us? Do we display the kind of characteristics that he valued? I said at the beginning, I think he's a genius but I'm not sure I'd want him for my boss. But would he even want you or me on his team? Did we list eight points about *him*? Try these on *you* for size:

1) The willingness to be totally committed to Christ is a starting point. But in your life, is that commitment to Christ matched by the next reason?
2) Are you aware that you don't know everything? Have there been occasions where you treated someone with the liberty that Paul showed Philemon? "I could order you, but instead I appeal, confident that the solution you come up with will be better than I could?"
3) Are you someone who could be thought of as courageous and a doer and someone who stands up to be counted when it means going against the grain?
4) Are you sacrificial in your leadership, willing to give up prestige, status, and being liked in order to embrace and wrestle with the difficult truths? What did you give up to become a Christian? Are there people that you wanted to like you or things you could have been but you had to let them go because you're a Christian?
5) Are you someone who listens deeply and understands deeply? Or, when you give advice, is that advice mostly about you and your standards and ideas rather than about the other person and their

situation? (As I indicated above, I probably do worst on this test.)
6) Do you listen in order to know what people will like, what will "sell," what will enhance your product, reputation, or self? Or do you listen past that to what is really needed? And do you offer the good rather than the popular, or do you try to overly sugarcoat?
7) Are you clever and creative when you communicate, conveying not what makes best sense to you but what will make most sense to your hearers? Are all your illustrative examples stories about you?
8) When you are forced into a position of justifying yourself, especially in comparison to another, do you talk about others as candidly and respectfully as Paul talks about Peter in Galatians and are you as complimentary in competition as Paul is in 1 Corinthians?

Would Paul like you? Think about all that you know about Paul now, and I believe you'll agree that if your answer to at least some of these questions is "I'd like to be that way," Paul would like you and be willing to work with you.

And oh, the letters he'd write to you!

And that's the key to using the Bible properly. Galatians wasn't written *to* us, exactly. But God caused it and all the other Scriptures to be written *for* us. Our job is to steep ourselves in it to the point that we know what was said in what situations in order to gain a three-dimensional picture, a model that allows us to think through what might have been written to us in our situations.

If the Corinthians had found a complete New Testament, their favorite book would have been Galatians ("Loosen up! It is for freedom Christ has set us free. Yay! Whee!"). You and I would now say to the Corinthians, "That was written to the Galatians, not to you Corinthians. You guys can't just take up what he writes without thinking how different their situation is from yours." Yet you and I do the same thing all the time. How can you and I be sure that our favorite Bible book – our favorite biblical advice – isn't just as seriously mis-applied?

Here's how: by reading it all and knowing the background questions and how they are like and unlike your own questions. Use those twin questions. What did it mean? What does it mean?

Remember my curator analogy from chapter 10: "Nudge the Renoir to the right"? We learn about straight and crooked from watching the curator adjust the paintings he nudges. It is not infrequently that we come to paintings that are crooked in the same way that one of his was, and we will nudge it exactly the same way. But even within the Bible, at least once Paul the curator said to a sub-curator, Philemon, "You are closer to the painting than I am. You can straighten it better by using the Christian principles I have taught you than by my trying to tell you which direction and how hard to nudge."

The Bible is not a book designed to be a reference answer book. The Bible is a book designed to change you and open you up to God and his Spirit within you – that Spirit who is a little like the horse who knows the way home. That's Christianity. Paul understands this. Think of it: Paul, who was once Saul, the expert in the Law, understands this.

C'mon; how can you not like such a guy?

Questions for Discussion or Reflection

1. What have I missed? What other reasons for liking Paul should I have added?

2. Reflect on/discuss other characters in the Bible that you think you should like but don't. Will you work on exploring one of them next?

3. Other biblical characters *should be* hard to like but don't seem to be – David, for instance, did lots of bad things. Why do we like him anyway? Should we?

Subject Index

Subject Index

seafood 127
selfishness 20–21
selflessness 107
sermons 3
servant 34, 38, 84, 90, 95, 106–107
sexuality 4, 70, 75, 78, 84, 86
shampoo 48
shirt 81
shoes 8
shortcuts 53
shotgun 69
Silas 7
sin 38, 49, 56, 78, 92
skepticism 95, 109
slavery 56, 58–59, 95–96, 101,
    113–114, 118–119, 121–124, 127,
    129–135, 140
snacks 75
society 4, 76, 91, 127, 130, 132–133
songs 37, 56, 115–116
sophists 74
soteriology (not used; see sanctification)
soul 38, 77–78, 118
speaking 3, 6, 12–14, 40, 52, 54, 72,
    76, 79, 96, 103, 109, 114, 116,
    130, 132, 141
Spirit, Holy 3, 34–35, 41, 43, 49–52,
    56, 58–60, 70, 84, 104, 146
spirit 38, 40, 78, 108, 110
spiritual 3, 57, 76, 78–81, 87–88, 109,
    134, 140
Stephanas 71, 77
Stephen 13, 15
stomach 78
student 3, 13–15, 20, 22, 33, 44–45,
    55, 84, 88, 98, 114, 117, 126

Stumpy-fingers (see John Mark) 6–7
submission 104
suffering 118
Supper, Lord's 68, 76, 80, 90, 101
surgery 57, 60
synagogue 46

tambourine 47
Tarsus 5, 11, 14–15
telephone 24, 32, 41, 45, 87
television 48
Temple (the Jewish one) 13–14, 17
temples 74–76, 84
temptation 41, 48, 87, 143
textbook 4, 44
texture 23–24, 54
thanks 36, 42–43, 54, 66, 89, 131, 142
theology 4, 45, 99–100, 109, 132
thief 113
throne 96
tongues 76, 79
toothbrushes 114
Torah 46, 50
tradition 11, 17, 36, 56, 88–90, 96–97,
    101
translation 21, 87–88, 113, 122
travel 6–7, 20, 67, 69, 77, 91
triangle 31, 50, 70
Trinity 83–84
Troas 6
tsk-tsk 106
tube 108

uh-huh 87
university 8, 11, 95
usury 130

vegetarianism 47

waiter 106
wardrobe 31
Wednesdays 21
witch 31
work 4, 6, 14, 34–35, 37–38, 50, 56,
    68–69, 74–75, 78–79, 83, 88,
    90–91, 94–95, 99, 101, 103,
    105–106, 108, 115, 122, 126,
    130–132, 134, 145, 147
worship 3, 15, 76, 79, 90, 93, 101, 105
wow 69, 119, 144
wrestle 144

yeah 87
yoke 95–96

Zakkai, Johannan ben 14
zeal 11–12, 16, 32, 34, 44, 47
zzzing 65

Scripture Index